THE BATTLE FOR THE WHITE HOUSE

... and the Soul of America

To All of My Irish and American Family

THE BATTLE FOR THE WHITE HOUSE

... and the Soul of America

Carole Coleman

The Liffey Press

Published by
The Liffey Press
Ashbrook House
10 Main Street, Raheny,
Dublin 5, Ireland
www.theliffeypress.com

A catalogue record of this book is
available from the British Library.

ISBN 978-1-905785-52-0

Printed in Ireland by Colour Books.

Contents

About the Author

Carole Coleman is a US-based freelance journalist who covered the 2008 US presidential election for "Today with Pat Kenny" on RTÉ Radio, and also contributes to BBC Radio and WAMU Radio in Washington DC. Carole was RTE's Washington correspondent from 2001–2005 and the station's Environment and Education correspondent from 1995–2000. The author of the best-selling book *Alleluia America: An Irish Journalist in Bush Country* (2005), she lives in Annapolis, Maryland.

Preface

WHEN I ARRIVED IN AMERICA as a journalist in 2001, there were three stories I wanted to cover. The first was the invisible wall of separation between the black and white populations. "It wouldn't have happened if we were white," I had heard two women say one evening on a Washington DC street. Though I didn't know what had happened to them, I wanted to know more about the young black women's lives. The second story was that, according to American advertisements, you can drive a new car off the lot with "No Money Down". It seemed too easy. My third story was how so few of the goods for sale in shops were "Made in America".

Soon terrorists attacked New York and Washington, and I quickly forgot about those stories. America first made strikes into the mountains of Afghanistan and then invaded Iraq. Old alliances fractured, American soldiers and foreign civilians died, and I had the opportunity to question the President of the United States about the wisdom of his decisions. For a time, being known as the journalist who challenged George W. Bush was a part of my identity.

Since I have stayed on in America, however, those early story ideas have come back to me in a more personal way. As a volunteer for our local Society of the St Vincent de Paul in my adopted hometown of Annapolis, Maryland, I see the struggles that keep so many African-Americans stuck in a cycle of poverty. As the "No Money Down" offers arrive in my mailbox, I too am often lured by the "Buy Now, Pay Later" economy. And like everyone else, my world is filled with Chinese-made goods.

In 2008, all these concerns came together in a perfect storm. American manufacturing hit its lowest level in a quarter century. A decade of crazy borrowing and unregulated financial markets ended abruptly with the Wall Street meltdown, and an African-American defied all expectations to win a marathon twenty-one-month race for the presidency.

I had already covered three previous US presidential elections, but the 2008 contest felt different from the very start. Before the candidates were even announced, Americans were busy debating their future. At workplaces, in colleges and among friends, politics was all the rage. Every election is fought on the promise of change, but this time, with fewer than one in three happy with the country's direction, the thirst for a new beginning was palpable.

I wrote this book to create a record of the epic battle for the White House that followed. I wrote it first and foremost for my own family, in the hope that some day maybe a niece or nephew will relive the incredible year I experienced from November 2007 to election day one year later. As a freelance journalist paying my own way, I travelled to several states, political rallies and conventions. I talked with each campaign's volunteers, their staffers when I could track them down, and individuals who knew the candidates before they ran for office. I drew on the wisdom of experts to interpret the events and the personalities. But mostly I enjoyed meeting with hundreds of ordinary voters. I did not have a vote, though in a quirk of the American system, a green card holder is permitted to donate thousands of dollars to a candidate. I did not contribute money to any of the candidates, and while asked to volunteer for just about all of them, I politely declined.

Wherever I went, I took my trusty tape recorder. From Charleston to Louisville, Des Moines to Baltimore, Little Rock to Chicago, I asked the same questions. "What's on your mind?" "Would you vote for a woman or a black man?" "How are you managing to get by in a worsening economy?" On weekends I drove to the battleground states of Pennsylvania and Virginia, visited the black neighbourhoods of downtown Baltimore, or just chatted with locals in Annapolis, Maryland.

Americans are ready for a new era of leadership. They are tired of mounting bills and stagnant wages, alarmed by illegal immigrants overwhelming their schools and hospitals, weary of war and being unloved abroad, and troubled by the increasing cost of health care and plummeting value of their homes. The forty-fourth president has a lot of soothing to do and a multitude of problems to tackle. Time will tell if he can live up to expectations, but the 2008 election turned a page in American history. Here's how I saw it unfold.

Carole Coleman
November 2008

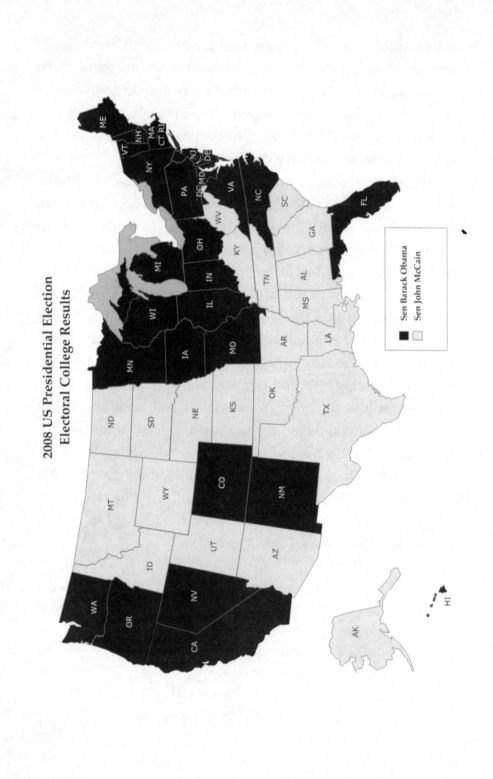

2008 US Presidential Election
Electoral College Results

Sen Barack Obama
Sen John McCain

1

Change Is in the Air

"There are some people that you meet in your life and you go, wow, he's going to go places." – OBAMA SUPPORTER

ON 4 NOVEMBER 2008 BARACK OBAMA was elected as the forty-fourth president of the United States. The landslide result was a clear rejection of policies that started deadly wars in Afghanistan and Iraq, produced steep economic decline and tarnished America's image throughout the world. Barack Obama's election also turned a page on the past where the American dream was not always the African-American reality. With the support of young people, minorities and ultimately a broad sweep of American voters, Obama and his simple message of "Change" outsmarted old political hands in both parties. This is my account of the longest, most dramatic and most significant election in recent American memory.

Let's begin in November 2007, a year before polling day, at the Jefferson Jackson dinner in Des Moines, Iowa. Dinner is perhaps too fancy a description for a hoedown in a stadium filled with 9,000 Democrats. Of those, 7,000, who had paid nothing, were crammed into the cold concrete stands and ordered to do plenty of cheering, while down on the floor the rest who had donated money to the political process gathered around tables for a chicken dinner and a bottle of beer. It was rough and ready, but in the heart of the Midwest, where the American presidential election kicks off every four years, this was the place to be.

One by one the Democratic Party hopefuls were called along with their partners to a platform in the centre of the stadium. By now political spouses had become as familiar as the candidates themselves. Too blonde, too bossy, too powerful – all were fair game for the critics. High up in the bleachers supporters chanted names, waved signs and made a racket – heralding the election antics to come. "Bi-den! Bi-den!" they shouted as the Delaware senator and second-time presidential candidate flashed the crowd his wide-angle grin.

Hillary Clinton came to dinner alone. Dressed in a dark brown business suit, she gave a high wave and pointed to a familiar face in the crowd. As the election progressed, I noticed that Clinton recognised someone in every crowd. Of course, most of the time there was no one there, but it gave her something to focus on while the cameras followed her about. "Turn up the heat!" her supporters yelled, signalling that the woman in the race was ready to kick it up a notch. Opinion polls showed her leading other candidates who had been campaigning in Iowa for a year. Former vice-presidential nominee John Edwards had been stumping here since 2006, whereas Connecticut senator Chris Dodd had moved his entire family to the state to impress the locals. But none could match Hillary Clinton's name recognition.

Bill Clinton was a no-show at the Iowa chicken dinner. The former president would have overshadowed his wife, fuelling the persistent theme that he was running for the White House again. Coming alone, Hillary showed that this was her campaign. But with just a few weeks left to the Iowa caucus, as the candidates posed on the platform with their partners, Hillary Clinton looked a bit awkward, as if she had forgotten something.

Barack Obama was the last to be announced. Just hearing his name set off the human equivalent of an earthquake in the stands, so powerful that you wondered if it was safe to remain inside. A thousand flashbulbs fired up the darkness as the lanky figure strode up the gangplank to the main stage. He was part boy, part politician, and for most people part mystery still to be unravelled. Behind him, Obama's long arm was outstretched to his wife Michelle, a woman as tall and angular as he was.

As they walked, this son of a Kenyan father and Kansan mother appeared to glide though a series of invisible barriers. The closer he got to the other candidates, the more the impediments of his race and youth fell away behind him. By the time he joined them on stage, his opponents looked outclassed, even vulnerable. The Obamas had the air of the Clintons when they were new to the national scene back in 1992, fresh and brimming with self-confidence. "Let us reach for what we know is possible," Obama told the crowd, "a nation healed, a world repaired, an America that believes again." Tonight, Hillary Clinton had left her old nineties rocker at home. Now she was dealing with not one but two rock stars. And they were black.

Concern over what had come to be known as "Clinton fatigue" was evident among Democrats in Iowa that night. "Do we really want thirty-two years of a Bush and a Clinton, followed by another Bush and another Clinton?" an elderly man asked, who then said that he had already decided to vote for Obama. Bill's undefined role in any new Clinton presidency was raising questions, and some feared the return of the personal dramas that had dominated the Clinton years. "Many times it seemed as if he was running for a third term," said author Sally Bedell Smith, who has chronicled the Clinton White House years. "I think he did see this as a way of redeeming himself through her presidency, kind of polishing his legacy and having a whole Clinton continuum that would be viewed by history as a success."

As far back as 2002 Hillary Clinton had worn the mantle of Democratic front-runner for president. That was even before John Kerry borrowed it to run against George W. Bush in 2004. The expectation that she would run was based on her successful transition from First Lady to senator, as well as the persistent Washington story that she and Bill had a pact – eight years for him and eight for her. "The notion of a Clinton succession has always been there," said Bedell Smith, though she was doubtful that there had been any agreement. "It was just part of their conversation that at some point she would have her turn." *Irish Voice* editor Niall O'Dowd, a key Clinton supporter, recalled that in 1998 he asked one of Hillary's confidants if she would run for president. "Does a bear shit in the woods?" the confidant replied.

Throughout George Bush's first term, the media tried to goad Hillary Clinton into running early. In September 2003, while she was meeting with then Taoiseach Bertie Ahern in Albany, New York, I took the opportunity to ask Mrs Clinton if she would challenge the sitting president. Though media speculation was building that she might throw her hat in the ring, she confirmed that a 2004 run was not her choice. "I've made my decision, and I see no reason to change it," Clinton said, explaining that her intent was to serve out her six-year term as the junior senator for New York before making any moves on the presidency.

It was the kind of open-ended answer that meant the press could start inquiring again after she was elected to a second Senate term in 2006. By then it was no secret that Clinton had begun fundraising and putting together lists of potential donors. The historic nature of a female candidacy only heightened the sense of anticipation. "People don't just like Hillary Clinton, they love her," Clinton's chief strategist Mark Penn wrote in a late 2006 memo unearthed by *The Atlantic*. Penn had suggested launching Clinton's presidential campaign in January 2007 with "blowout" trips to Iowa and New Hampshire.

So that January, twenty-two months before the election, Clinton used a webcast to announce what most of the world already knew. "I'm in. And I'm in to win!" Clinton said, beginning what she called a "conversation" with Americans. But the party's newest star had already beaten her to it. Just days earlier, Barack Obama had confirmed his candidacy. Obama's decision was arrived at more quickly, the result of nudging from political colleagues and discussion with his wife Michelle. Weeks later he made a formal address from the steps of the State House in Springfield, Illinois. Choosing the same spot where Abraham Lincoln had once said, "A house divided against itself cannot stand," Barack Obama began his quest to harness a nation bitterly divided over the direction America should take at home and abroad.

If Hillary Clinton had challenged George W. Bush in 2004, the trajectory of Obama's rise to the White House might have been different. As an Illinois state senator eyeing higher office, Obama was in the final stages of a run for the US Senate in November 2004 when John Kerry gave him the break he had been waiting for. Kerry had selected Obama to present the keynote address at the Democratic convention in Boston. It was the first time a national audience would be moved by Obama's personal story. "My parents shared an improbable love. They shared an abiding faith in the possibilities of this nation. They would give me an African name, Barack or 'blessed', believing that in a tolerant America your name is no barrier to success," he said.

But what made Obama an instant sensation in Boston was his vision of a unified America at a time when "Red" and "Blue" seemed to be at each other's throats. "The pundits like to slice and dice our country into Red states and Blue states, Red states for Republicans and Blue states for Democrats. But I say to them tonight there is not a liberal America and a conservative America – there is the United States of America. There is not a black America and a white America and a Latino America and an Asian America – there is a United States of America."

Obama's idealistic vision and fresh face immediately catapulted him onto the national political stage. Though still a state senator, the self-described "skinny kid with the funny name" was being mentioned as a future president. Within weeks of the Boston speech, Obama was elected to the Senate in a landslide victory that brought him one step closer to the centre of power. Hillary Clinton was among those who had helped Obama get there, having opened her home in Washington to host a fundraiser for her fellow Chicagoan.

When they faced each other in Iowa three years later, Barack Obama was still a Washington rookie. Out of the fifty

Democratic senators then in office, he was ranked forty-ninth in seniority. Clinton was thirty-sixth. The only thing they had in common was that they both travelled now with Secret Service protection, the only two presidential candidates to do so. Clinton was protected as a former First Lady, and Obama was assigned security in 2007 to deal with growing crowds and unspecified threats. But with his complicated biography and scant experience, even those who doubted Clinton would become president were ambivalent about Obama's chances of beating her to the nomination. Only people close to Barack Obama knew he could pull it off. "He told me he would either be president or the greatest civil rights lawyer ever," said Linda Randle, a community activist who had worked with Obama in Chicago in the 1980s. It had been twenty years, she said, since he had made that prediction, but now here he was. "There are some people that you meet in your life and you go, wow, he's going to go places!"

"Why will you win in Iowa?" I asked Obama at a farmers' meeting in Des Moines the morning before the Jefferson Jackson dinner as he canvassed for the crucial first caucus vote.

"Because I have all these wonderful people here," Obama said, gesturing to the group of mainly middle-aged men and women who had got out of their beds to hear him speak about something he didn't know much about – cows and corn subsidies. "We're spending a lot of time with them. I believe in them, so I think they'll believe in me," he said. It wasn't the most illuminating answer, but as it turned out, the time the Obama campaign spent in Iowa paid huge dividends.

Yet despite Obama's star status at the Jefferson Jackson event, the nomination was still Clinton's to lose. On learning that she was staying at the same suburban Des Moines hotel that I had booked into, I tried to engineer an encounter. More and more she was dodging the press, confining herself to a well-insulated bubble that aides had created and maintained with the help of around-the-clock security.

The candidate and her personal staff were occupying three or four rooms on the top floor at the hotel. Secret Service personnel were patrolling the corridor outside room 1021 and, as luck would have it, my room was just doors away. When simply waiting for her to emerge didn't work, I wrote a letter asking if she might have a few minutes to talk about her plans and the importance of her Irish support base.

The best chance for what journalists call a "big get" is generally in a quiet area away from the press pack. Bill Clinton was due to travel to Dublin the following weekend to attend a private fundraiser for his wife's campaign, so it seemed like the stars might be aligned. Sitting on my bed, I dared to picture Hillary and myself chatting in the hotel room three doors away about her plans to win the nomination.

My handwritten letter was accepted by a member of the Secret Service, who passed it to one of Mrs Clinton's aides. He may or may not have shown it to the candidate, but I was never called to Room 1021 and about two hours later they had all checked out of the hotel. The only evidence that remained of the Clinton entourage was a tray of half-eaten hamburgers outside Hillary Clinton's room. No one had seen the front-runner leave.

I should not have been disappointed. The campaign's strategy was to limit Clinton's media exposure to avoid unnecessary slip-ups. But Obama's reception at the Jefferson Jackson dinner the previous night may also have jolted the Clinton team. In the following weeks local polls showed both Barack

Obama and John Edwards pulling equal with Hillary Clinton in Iowa. Clinton's commanding lead was evaporating, and it would be a three-way battle for the first electoral prize of the primary season.

Unlike Clinton, John Edwards was happy to face the media, with some exceptions. "Refusing donations from lobbyists seems to be working for you," I said, when I caught up with Edwards later that day in Des Moines.

"Where are you from?" he inquired.

"Ireland," I said, as Edwards settled into a lengthy answer about all the dirty money sloshing around American politics.

"What about the future US policy on NATO?" a reporter behind me asked.

"Where are you from?" Edwards asked, noting another accent.

"Germany."

"I don't think there are any votes in Germany," he remarked, before turning on his heel and leaving. John Edwards eventually dropped out of the race after a disappointing showing and endorsed Barack Obama.

With just weeks to go in Iowa, Hillary Clinton deployed a strike force of extra staff to try to retake the momentum. But while her planners had been engaged elsewhere on the electoral map, the Obama ground crew, led by Paul Tewes, had been busy peddling Obama's "Change" message door-to-door. Rory Finnin, who volunteered with the Obama team, recalled a conference call with Paul Tewes days before the caucus. "There was a poll from the *Des Moines Register* newspaper showing Barack Obama with a five per cent lead over John Edwards. I remember him vividly saying, 'Polls don't mean shit,' repeatedly over and over on this conference call." Tewes wanted his people out on the streets making sure nobody was left sitting at home on caucus night. "He was very vocal about making sure we stuck to our plan and forgot the polls."

On 3 January 2008 Iowans confirmed what appeared obvious on the night in the Des Moines stadium. Barack Obama became the first black man to win Iowa in a presidential primary. Though Obama had visualised this victory over a year earlier and engineered it with the help of a committed network of supporters, he knew he had defied the expectations of not only most Americans but of the world. "They said this day would never come," Obama said, and without using the words "race" or "black", he described that January night in America as "the moment when we tore down barriers that have divided us for too long".

"They always say we can't do anything," an elderly black woman told me, explaining how Barack Obama's success in 2008 had helped to improve the self-image of every African-American. "That's not true any more," I said. "It never was," she corrected me. "We are CEOs of major corporations, we are doctors, lawyers. We are not just athletes. We are everything. But they never gave us that credit."

Obama won 38 per cent of the Iowa vote, handily beating John Edwards, who came in second with 30 per cent. Hillary Clinton, the presumptive front-runner, had to settle for third place. In Des Moines that night Mrs Clinton put on a brave smile, but it was the faces beside her that spoke volumes. Bill Clinton looked red and wistful, as if he wanted to be somewhere else quickly. And Madeleine Albright, the former Secretary of State, appeared as though she had been dragged up from the past to illustrate that the Clintons were the ageing Democratic establishment and Obama was the future.

"I mean, the shock in the headquarters! People were devastated. They were just so surprised," explained Caitríona Fitzpatrick, a postgraduate student from Cork who started as an intern at Clinton campaign headquarters on the day of the Iowa result. It was bad enough arriving at a drab, windowless building in Arlington, Virginia, formerly used for processing immigrants, but having to join a team stunned into disbelief was an auspicious start for Caitríona. "You are in a real bubble," she said of the war room mentality inside a political campaign, where only positive vibes and good news were encouraged. "I found myself getting into it. When I would ring home, they would have a totally different spin on what was happening to what I would have working there."

The Iowa result shifted the political plates in a way rarely seen in America. Workplaces and homes were abuzz with conversations about what it all meant, and the airwaves crackled to sounds of a new theme tune. "Hope" and "Change" quickly became the slogans of Obama's campaign for the White House.

After years of an unpopular administration, everyone was promising change but with Obama it just took off. "It caught on because of him," said Patrick Lewis, Deputy Director of Veterans Outreach for Hillary Clinton. "Change" would become a lot easier to define against a Republican opponent. But what was undeniable from the start was that Obama embodied the word. Barack Obama looked like "Change".

Obama had also ridden to his first primary victory on a tide of disaffected youth. From Cedar Rapids to the bridges of Madison County, young volunteers had manned phone banks and handed out leaflets eighteen hours a day. College students, many of whom were still on Christmas break during the Iowa caucus, returned early to help and to vote. Having been raised on a diet of Clinton dramas and George W. Bush's so-called "reign of error", students across the country were looking for a new direction.

"Definitely Obama!" said Lauren Fuller, a student at James Madison University in Virginia, who told me she was sick of listening to candidates talking about patriotism yet never delivering on the important issues. "He actually talks to the voters like they are intelligent people," she said of Obama. Others, like Kyle Bonnifer from New York, were drawn by Obama's ability to inspire. "I don't think it's as much his policies as his charisma and public speaking skills." Whatever the attraction, Iowa students learned about the caucus system so they could help out on polling day.

What separates a caucus meeting from a straight ballot box vote is that you can enter a caucus intending to vote for one candidate and leave having voted for another. There is an element of persuasion involved, and Obama's people were primed to persuade. His "ground crew" mastered the basics and even held mock meetings, so that when the real thing began they were first out of the traps to make the case for Obama. This was crucial in winning over voters who initially supported candidates eliminated in the first round. Such voters were then free to choose another candidate.

Following the Iowa bombshell, speculation was rife about the health of the Clinton campaign. Cable channels such as MSNBC, which dominate election coverage inside the US, seemed giddy at the prospect of seeing the "queen of polls" toppled in such a dramatic fashion. "I think they wanted to beat up on Hillary," said Bill Silcock, a professor at the Walter Cronkite School of Journalism in Arizona. "Obama was the sexier candidate." But they were too happy, laughing even.

Some newspapers were already reporting the race in a way that was clearly tilted away from her, if not already looking beyond her. "The media were proud of the fact that it wasn't a done deal. That made it exciting," said Silcock.

What America witnessed next was the Clintons in survival mode. Every biographical study of the duo illustrates that they are at peak performance when under the most intense pressure. With just five days between Iowa and the next big contest on the primary calendar in New Hampshire, pollsters were measuring opinion twice daily. They might as well have been checking Clinton's pulse. And the closer it came to polling day, the more they believed that the patient's strength was ebbing. On the eve of the New Hampshire vote, one poll had Obama winning by as much as 13 per cent. Even Clinton's own pollster had her down 11 per cent. Only local journalists urged the obituary writers to keep their ink in the bottle.

Hillary Clinton's arrival at a freezing cold airport hangar in Nashua, New Hampshire, just hours after the humiliating third-place finish in Iowa, signalled her determination to make up for it. "I am so ready for the rest of this campaign, and I am so ready to lead!" Clinton declared, as she plunged into long days, pressing every palm, visiting every diner and promising voters she would fight for them every day in office.

No one doubted her capacity to fight, or what one voter famously described as her "testicular fortitude". From the beginning, Hillary Clinton had run a man's campaign, playing down her feminine side. Rather than presenting herself as a woman in a man's game, Clinton came across as one who had already cracked the male code. "Her father insisted that she play baseball with the boys. He told her that to understand how men think, you start off by playing the sports they are interested in,"

Hillary's old high school teacher Paul Carlson had explained to me when I visited her home town, Park Ridge, Illinois.

Hillary Rodham had begun her career as a lawyer seeking justice and better educational opportunities for women and children. But when she stood against an all-male line-up for the top political job, it was her experience in foreign affairs and her knowledge of governing that she wanted to stress. Being the first woman president was merely a helpful historic tag, not a psychology to be mined for womanly advantages. Mark Penn saw Margaret Thatcher as the best role model for her. "She represents the most successful elected woman leader in this century, and the adjectives that were used about her (Iron Lady) were not of good humour or warmth," he wrote in a 2006 memo to Hillary Clinton. "As we move forward it is important to understand who we are and who we are not. We are more Thatcher than anyone else."

Yet the moment when Hillary began to fight back tears in a town hall meeting in Portsmouth, New Hampshire, she became a vulnerable woman again. It was a display of human frailty so significant that within hours Clinton had stormed back to victory, turning around her fortunes for the first time.

"As a woman, I know it's hard to get out of the house in the morning. How do you do it?" inquired Marianne Pernold-Young, a sixty-four-year-old local photographer who had dropped into the meeting and was curious to know how the candidate kept it all together. Clinton, who turned sixty the previous October, had been criss-crossing the country for a year attending three or four public events a day. "It's not easy, and I couldn't do it if I just didn't passionately believe it was the right thing to do," Clinton sighed, sitting on the edge of a stage where she had answered policy questions for two hours.

Clinton's head was in her hands, and her voice was beginning to crack. "You know, I have so many opportunities from this country. I just don't want to see us fall backwards," Hillary said, her eyes misting up. "This is very personal for me. It's not just political."

"She looked at me straight in the face, like a girlfriend, and I said, 'Holy Toledo, what just happened?'" Marianne told me later. "The media were saying I cracked her, and she didn't even crack when her husband was cheating on her."

Coincidence or not, Hillary defied both polls and pundits to win the New Hampshire primary. With help from women, Clinton's bid for the presidency had been rescued from a premature end. "I found my own voice," she declared. But Marianne Pernold-Young, who had helped her find it, did not vote for her. "Obama made me cry," Marianne explained. "I want someone new who doesn't owe any favors to anybody. I believe he's going to open the windows and let fresh air into the White House. He's going to let new things happen," said Pernold-Young.

AMIDST ALL THE THEATRE THAT FIRST week in January 2008, the Republican primaries were like a circus sideshow. John McCain, whose presidential bid was still recovering from a near death experience the previous summer, barely bothered to campaign in Iowa. The war hero and twenty-six-year veteran of Washington politics had met a dead-end, which left him broke and without staff. But McCain found new advisers and fashioned a fresh strategy, focusing his energy upon the New Hampshire primary. If he could win big there, McCain figured, he'd be on his way.

While McCain's campaign struggled to remake itself, Rudy Giuliani had emerged as the Republican front-runner. The former New York mayor ran on the issue of security, hoping to use his 9/11 persona as the man who held the city's hand on its darkest day to carry him to Washington. For a while it seemed to work. Everyone in America had heard of Rudy. But the New York press had gone cool on him, highlighting the millions of dollars Giuliani had made from his security businesses since the terrorist attacks and a personal life fraught with difficulty. "If his own kids won't talk to him, how can we trust him to run the country?" was how one voter in Annapolis, Maryland, put it. Rudy Giuliani would spend $50 million – betting most of it on Florida which he lost to John McCain at the end of January 2008.

Mike Huckabee was the surprise candidate for the Republicans in 2008. Originally from Hope, Arkansas, the same town as Bill Clinton, Huckabee had also served as his state's governor. "He was a good governor, but people won't vote for him because he's got good moral standards," a Little Rock construction worker volunteered when I visited there in November 2007. Like President Bill Clinton, Mike Huckabee was a natural with people and he could knock a tune out of a bass guitar. But Huckabee was also a former pastor who had once suggested that AIDS sufferers needed to be locked up – an extreme view that appealed mainly to the right wing of the Republican Party.

John McCain's other main competition came from a self-made Mormon multi-millionaire. Many voters felt that Mitt Romney, a businessman and former Massachusetts governor, was the candidate best qualified to turn around the ailing US economy. Romney looked presidential and performed well in debates, but by January he was financing his own campaign while others were raising millions from supporters. The actor and former senator Fred Thompson also threw his hat in the ring but failed to measure up to the hopes of those searching for a new Ronald Reagan.

While Barack Obama had won the Democratic contest in Iowa, Mike Huckabee took the Republican prize and continued as a colourful presence in the race for several months afterwards. But over in New Hampshire, where Hillary was eyeing a comeback, John McCain was also retrieving his confidence. McCain's support for the "surge" of extra troops into Iraq in the spring of 2007 was paying off, as reports suggested that Iraq was becoming more secure and US troop fatalities were down. The man known as the "Maverick" won easily, and his "Straight Talk Express" campaign bus left New Hampshire with John McCain the Republican front-runner once again.

BY ONLY THE SECOND WEEK IN January, both Joe Biden and Chris Dodd had dropped out of the Democratic race. John Edwards was still hanging on, but it had effectively become a battle between Hillary Clinton and the inspirational newcomer with a Muslim-sounding name. "Obarama," "Barakama" and "that black guy" were amongst versions I heard from voters around the country. The Clinton campaign in some of its internal memos even referred to Obama as "BHO" – Barack Hussein Obama – his given name.

If I had met Hillary Clinton that November day in Room 1021, I would never have thought to ask her if she could have imagined she would someday urge her supporters to vote for Obama for President. "It was so inconceivable – and it probably still is to a lot of people there – that she wouldn't get in," said Caitríona Fitzpatrick, referring to her former colleagues inside the Clinton campaign. "They didn't really think that Obama would overtake her."

I certainly never would have thought to inquire if Clinton could see herself asking Obama to help pay off her campaign debt. Such a question might have got me seen to the door. We didn't know then that Hillary Clinton would end up broke, and that a forty-four-year-old from the North Slope of Alaska whose target voter was "Joe Six-Pack" would become the woman of attention in the race. But this was all part of what made the 2008 American presidential election one for the comedians, as well as the history books.

2

Fairytale of South Carolina

"The same hands that used to pick cotton in South Carolina will have the opportunity to pick the next president of the United States." – DR LONNIE RANDOLPH

JUST ABOUT 13 PER CENT OF the US population is African-American. But to have any understanding of Black America, you should travel south. It is not that the black population elsewhere won't open up if you ask, but with all the awkward self-consciousness and politically correct jargon surrounding race, it's hard to know where to begin with someone whose skin tone governs so much in their lives.

"What's it like, you know, being black? Or, sorry, should I say African-American?"

Whenever the opportunity presented itself, the questions would come flooding into my head, but I could never get them out of my mouth. Asking someone how it feels to be a second-class citizen is hardly the stuff of casual conversation on the underground in Washington DC, where I have often been the only white face on the train. Nor does it make for a fun night out, not that any of the black friends I have made in America ever bother with the downtown bars and restaurants that white people frequent.

My introduction to African-Americans was through a black cameraman called Ted, who I had worked with in Florida during the 2000 election recount battle between George W. Bush and Al Gore. Hotel rooms in Tallahassee, where the courts were arguing the case, were booked out, so we rented a house for a couple of nights about thirty miles out in the countryside. We had just filmed a news story for RTÉ. It was late and we were both hungry. When I asked Ted where he would like to go to eat, he shook his head. He wouldn't eat out in the area where we were staying, he said, because it was not his kind of place. I listened to his explanation.

It would not be a good idea for a black man, Ted felt, to be seen with a white woman in what was a rural white conservative part of America. Even though we had spent the day working together as professionals, he was afraid to share a table with me in a rural Florida restaurant. We were in the twenty-first century, yet that night I felt as though I had stepped back into the Old South. We stayed in for the evening, ate crisps, drank beer and talked. "Have you read *Uncle Tom's Cabin*?" Ted asked, after we had opened our second six-pack. I hadn't then, but he assured me that the segregationist ideas behind the Jim Crow laws had not gone away. There was a deep frustration behind his normally bright smile and a palpable anger over the unresolved hurt still felt by black Americans. To the outside world, Ted had risen above the expectations of so many of his peers to make a success of his life, but how much had really been achieved when this young black professional still felt more comfortable hiding indoors than to be seen dining with a white woman?

Fast forward to January 2008 in Charleston, South Carolina. It was the weekend of the annual Martin Luther King Day holiday and just days before the state's Democratic presidential primary. Former First Lady Hillary Clinton was still the national front runner, but she was locked in a fierce battle with Illinois Senator Barack Obama. Weeks earlier, Obama had swept to victory in Iowa, uncorking something both new and old in American culture – race. Like the genie escaping from a bottle, Obama had given black America the moderate hopeful voice it had been missing since Dr King's assassination exactly forty years earlier.

In the days after Iowa I walked the streets of Baltimore, Maryland, talking with black Americans. Obama could never be president they told me. Sure he was a great candidate, and they were so darn proud. But there was just too much prejudice around for that to happen. "A black man is not going to be as powerful in there as a white man," one woman reasoned, referring to the White House. "They might try to hurt him. His life might be on the line." It was old entrenched thinking, based on fear, and it would take more than one happy result to change it. To African-Americans, President Bill Clinton was the leader who had communicated most effectively with them, and except for the younger people, most voters I spoke to that day were voting for Hillary Clinton.

Two weeks later, a 180 degree shift had taken place. Obama's close second in New Hampshire and his inspirational words had convinced millions of African-Americans that maybe he could win after all. "Yes we can," he told them, and it got them thinking that this long skinny fellow, even if he was only "half a brother" given that his mother had been a white woman, just might represent the change they craved.

The locals I saw on the way into the southern city of Charleston looked as if they could do with some change. Black youths with expressionless faces hung out around street corners, propping up houses that seemed ready to crumble if the youngsters stepped away from them. In the January chill, women lugged groceries from the shops, while girls in skin-tight jeans and coppery hairdos lumbered up the sidewalk in impossibly high heels. Young mothers were trailed by miniature versions of the corner boys, and by tiny girls in pink tracksuits with corn rows that must have taken hours to braid into their hair. For several blocks I cruised past the grim real estate that identifies so much of black America. Then it ended, and the city I recognised from the tourist brochures began.

Downtown Charleston is situated on a peninsula that juts east to the Atlantic Ocean. On one side is the Cooper River and on the other the Ashley River. A big deep port made it the ideal place for the transportation of goods and people. Today, that fact is a vital part of the city's cultural and economic history. Charleston was a major port of entry for African slaves being brought to America.

Yards beyond the edge of the modern ghetto is one of the country's most impressive neighbourhoods. Above the sidewalk, the grand houses of the Old South rise majestically. The Calhoun and Aiken-Rhett mansions still use the cobblestone entryways where horse-drawn coaches once pulled up to drop off their passengers. Behind wrought iron gates and original glass windows sit antiques and artefacts that bear witness to two centuries of social division. You can just about hear the lady of the house calling out to her black maid to bring up some more sweet tea.

The switch in African-American support from the Clintons to Barack Obama that occurred here during the last weeks of February 2008 was swift and aided somewhat by Bill Clinton, who hit the campaign trail after his wife's loss in Iowa. The former president charged into South Carolina like a bull. He snarled at reporters who approached him and threw several red-faced fits while attempting to force-feed re-heated 1990s' fare to an electorate who had already got a whiff of something fresh being cooked up.

Assuming the role of campaign attack dog, Bill Clinton picked apart Obama's statements against the Iraq war, while Hillary dumped cold water on comparisons between her rival and the civil rights leader Martin Luther King. "It took a president to get it done," she declared, claiming that while Dr King had fired up the civil rights movement, President Lyndon Johnson had signed the 1964 Civil Rights Act. It was certainly true that Johnson had sacrificed his own popularity to push through the legislation, and that his wife Lady Bird Johnson had been cursed by whites as she toured the South trying to sell the changes. Still, any diminution of the role played by the slain Dr King was an affront to black leaders. James Clyburn, the powerful South Carolina congressman and House Majority Whip, encouraged candidates to be "sensitive about the words they use". Bill Clinton, once dubbed "America's first black president" for his unique ability to communicate with African-Americans, was rapidly losing that connection.

The backlash against Bill Clinton, according to Max Brantley, an old friend of the Clintons and editor of the *Arkansas Times*, was part of a concerted strategy by the Obama campaign to stir the black base for their candidate. "It was feigned offence at the speaking of fact," said Brantley, who believed

Bill Clinton's comment – that Obama would probably win South Carolina because Jessie Jackson had previously won the Democratic primary there – was blown out of proportion. "It was viewed as ungracious of Bill Clinton to say that. The good sport in American politics says we got whooped. But was it a racist comment? It didn't seem so to me. On the other hand, I'm not a black person." In Bill Clinton's mind, according to Brantley, part of his legacy is that he was a post-racial president. "He made meaningful strides by including diverse sorts of people in his administration, going way back to his beginnings as an Arkansas politician."

But Clinton also found himself in trouble when he used the word "fairytale" to describe Barack Obama's record on the Iraq war. Though Obama had been against the war before it began in 2003, he voted to continue funding it when he got to Washington in 2004. This shifting stance prompted Bill Clinton to describe Obama's anti-war record as "the biggest fairytale I've ever heard". But once this particular f–word got caught up in the media cyclone, it quickly became interpreted as a slur on Barack Obama's entire candidacy and all who supported it. As one accusation led to another, and each unintended smear and innuendo compounded the next, African-Americans parted company with the Clintons and joined Obama's caravan of hope that was moving through the state at breakneck speed.

THE RAIN WAS COMING DOWN in buckets as the Reverend Joseph Darby ushered me into his church by a side door on Charleston's Morris Street. I followed him into a small wood-panelled room where he reclined in a brown leather chair and rested his feet on the waste basket. "I just had Bill Clinton on here," he said, throwing his eye toward the telephone on his desk. "You know, it's the only time I have ever got to speak with a president, and I told him off!" Darby laughed at his own audacity. Clinton had been hoping to limit any damage with local church leaders. None of the comments of recent days, he told Darby, had been intended to cause any racial hurt. Clinton simply felt that voters of all colours needed to stick with the candidate who had a proven record for getting things done.

But the forty-second president had missed the whole point of the South Carolina primary. Barack Obama was important there because of what he symbolised. He held out hope for a third of the state's population, the 1.4 million blacks who felt held back by an invisible yet potent force. Even if he didn't make it all the way to the Oval Office, Obama had already played a role that stretched beyond mere presidential politics. He had inspired people and got them interested again. The Reverend Darby dismissed the argument, popular with the media at the time, that Obama wasn't black enough to earn the trust of real "brothers". "Most African-Americans are the product of mixed race," he said. "Look at me. Darby is Irish, which means that at some point in my mother's lineage, as she was a Gilleret, there had to have been a voluntary or an involuntary mixed relationship."

Darby didn't mince words when it came to the pain that still defines the contours of the American South. For thirty years he had been preaching it from the pulpit of this very church. Now, he and thousands of pastors in churches across the South were finally being heard. What they had to report was that while civil rights laws had improved their lives, they had not changed hearts and minds.

"Segregation is not legal any more in South Carolina, but racial prejudice is alive and well," Darby said, explaining how it continues to permeate throughout education, health care and housing. "No one would intentionally segregate housing these days, but it's a lot easier for white South Carolinians to get a house than for black South Carolinians. Loans tend to be more expensive and far easier to lose to foreclosure," he explained, pointing out that if city authorities wanted to clear an area of poor blacks, they simply raised local property values so residents would not be able to afford annual house taxes. That's why his African-American church was now in the middle of a white residential area. The word "segregation", Darby said, was no longer in use in Charleston, a city he described as infected with "raging politeness". "That's how the American South has dealt with the issue of race – by not talking about it."

This deep reservoir of frustration made the sudden lure of change irresistible to those still willing to give politics a shot. "Change" was the current jargon. But looking at the sea of black faces at Obama rallies that weekend, I wondered how much weight a single word could carry with people who had been promised change before, only to be left behind.

"Change." The reverend Darby kicked at the waste basket as he turned around the word in his head. "There's a wonderful lyric by the late James Brown that says, 'I don't want nobody to give me nothing. Just open the door and I'll get it myself.' I think the basic desire is that there be equal opportunity."

Darby was still wanting to talk, but I headed back out into the rain. We agreed that I would have to come back again.

IT WAS ALL RAGING POLITENESS THE following morning as a smiling blonde lady handed me a plate. "All this good food will go to waste," she said, explaining that people at her breakfast meeting had a lunch to get off to, so they didn't eat much. She gestured to a large display of American breakfast fare – chocolate muffins, fruit cocktail and cans of Diet Coke. I had just wandered in, but I poured a soft drink and we talked about accents, religion and family ties. Barbara was a walking billboard for southern charm. Unlike her northern sisters, she was not in a hurry. She moved slowly and deliberately, smiled a lot, and spoke with the silky smooth drawl of a fifties movie star. Like every white southerner I had ever run into, Barbara was on a mission. Hers was to raise money for Citadel scholarships.

The Citadel, America's oldest private military college, is located at the northern end of Charleston's peninsula and looks like a castle that has escaped from a fairytale. Its exterior walls enclose a large central square, where neat figures dressed in starched blue uniforms dart in and out of doors and alleyways. As I drove through the campus, a game of American football was being played in the pouring rain.

The Citadel is not a reform school, but the programme does instil patriotism, academic perfection and a fighting spirit in its charges. First year students, who get the full blast of indoctrination, are known as "knobs", and rigid discipline is designed to build lifelong camaraderie among those subjected to it. The clear implication is that you will not forget your time here, and your classmates will not either. Memories of starched military uniforms and sopping wet football games will bind you together in old age.

Politics is not a taboo subject inside the castle walls, and the party of choice is the Grand Old Party – the more colloquial name for Republicans. On that morning the college alumni centre was being wired for sound and video to accommodate John McCain's expected victory in the day's South Carolina Republican primary. It would be a sweet success for the man who had lost to George W. Bush here in 2000. That primary had been a bitter contest, during which false rumours were spread by Bush supporters that John McCain had fathered a black child. The child in question was the McCains' daughter Brigit, an orphan the couple adopted from Bangladesh.

"What's eight years among friends?" Senator McCain said as he arrived at the Citadel to cement his status as the Republican Party frontrunner in the 2008 primary election.

"Mac is back! Mac is back!" supporters cheered, as the banks of television cameras flickered to life and sent their signals racing through the lines until we could see ourselves on Fox News. On stage, the candidate was joined by his wife Cindy and mother Roberta, a lively-looking ninety-six-year-old who appeared regularly throughout the 2008 campaign to remind Americans that the McCain genes were bankable. At seventy-two, the oldest candidate to ever run for the White House, the senator was still Roberta McCain's baby.

The political signal beamed out that night from the Citadel was that America needed to remain on the offensive in its war on terror. By now, McCain's favourite stump line was that he would rather "win a war and lose an election" if that's what it took to see the Iraq mission through. Again the crowd gave it up for Mac – a steadfast supporter of the late surge of extra troops into Iraq, a decorated Vietnam War hero and an American patriot. "We're military down here," an elderly woman shouted into my ear to make sure I understood the significance of the primary result. "We've been involved in every major conflict up to now, and we hope we will continue to be."

In a way it was a simple matter of survival. If there were no wars to fight, there might not be any need for a strong military. If that were the case, there might not be a big Air Force base by the Charleston airport. There might not be training and proving grounds along the Cooper and Ashley Rivers – and maybe no Citadel. As much as any other industry, life in this part of South Carolina relied on the machinery and pageantry of war. Nagging doubts about the foolishness of the Iraq invasion could easily be put to rest when the local economy depended on having at least a hint of a conflict on the horizon.

ALPHONSO BROWN, A GREAT-GRANDSON of African slaves, gulped a soda as he sat in the driver's seat of his plush air-conditioned minibus in the centre of Charleston. It was a half-hour before his next run, but already tourists were lining up at the door looking to be transported back to the days when white men were legal owners of black men, women and children. "Slave life, that's what they want me to show them! Why would I want to go back to that?" he chuckled. "They're looking for the authentic experience, but it's gone."

Alphonso spoke with the musical cadence that shapes his peculiar dialect. Gullah is a Creole language that slaves in this area concocted while trying to master English. Gullah was once widely spoken in coastal parts of North and South Carolina, especially in Charleston, where even white children learned it from their black nannies. "Our ancestors were not trying to hold on to anything. They were trying to speak English," Brown said. As a child Alphonso himself had been teased for his "bad English," because after school was over, he returned home to where only Gullah was spoken. "The English you hear me speaking now has been practised," Brown said, explaining that he had gone to college and become a teacher.

As slaves, his own great-grandparents worked to better their lives, an impulse Brown claimed was presently missing in

Charleston's black youngsters. "There are more black youth in jail now than there are in college," he announced sadly as tourists filed into the bus.

"Could an election really bring 'Change you can believe in?'" I asked, searching for his thoughts on the power of politics to reverse the negative trends of recent decades.

"Not unless a president has a strong Congress on his side," Alphonso Brown said. "It's the congressmen who make the laws in Washington, not the president."

AFTER TWO DAYS IN CHARLESTON, IT WAS time to travel inland. South Carolina's capital, Columbia, it was often argued, still clung to an overt form of racial bigotry. It is not a distinction that any other state would be keen to emphasise, but here the local government liked to run this particular flag up the pole – literally. In 2008, on the grounds of South Carolina's State House, a Confederate flag was still blowing in the wind.

In the eight years since I had first come to the United States, there had been numerous dust-ups over this display. The local government defended it as an important symbol of states that in 1860 had gone to war with Union troops in the North. But the American Civil War is also widely acknowledged to have been about the right of southern slave-owners to continue regarding people as property. These days the Confederacy has spawned waves of nostalgia for the Old South and its gentlemen generals like Robert E. Lee. For millions of Americans the flag is a popular symbol of that time. While freedom of speech allows any individual to display the Confederate flag on private property, the decision by the state government to fly this flag so prominently is seen as an affront to the state's large black population. After years of protests and legal challenges, the flag was removed from the top of the State House dome but still flies on the Capitol grounds.

On the morning of Martin Luther King Day, I grabbed the last spot on the media platform in front of the Capitol. Directly above us, the Confederate flag flapped about in the icy cold breeze. At its base, groups of black teenagers shivered in their oversized clothes and baggy pants. They had gathered for the annual reminder that Dr King, a brother from Georgia, had once lifted them up almost high enough to tear down the symbols that continue to offend them and to dismantle the hurt built up over generations.

From my perch I noticed a growing commotion on the street opposite the State House. A media scrum had developed near the front of an approaching march, with television cameras jostling for an opening in the crowd. When I got a clearer view, I saw the unmistakable head of Barack Obama. He was striding up the street in his long black coat, flanked by black leaders and trailed by a throng of chanting locals. Obama was one of three Democratic presidential candidates in town to address the crowd that day, but he was the highlight. In Barack Obama, these shivering black teenagers were searching for the modern incarnation of a hero they had never known.

I had often wished to be transported back to the 1960s to see and to feel what had gone on in the South. That January morning in Columbia was as close as I would ever get. "I remember having to sit at the back of the bus," a woman in her sixties told me, and as the speakers got up to address the crowd, it almost felt as though the civil rights movement had never ended.

"No state that respects its people would fly a symbol of white supremacy here," howled Dr Lonnie Randolph. As leader of the National Association for the Advancement of Colored

People (NAACP) in South Carolina he was not pulling any punches. "That's right," replied voices from the crowd. I stole a glance at the Confederate flag which was now limp in the morning sun. For the next ten minutes Randolph ran through a litany of facts which left no doubt as to why America's black population was about to turn to Barack Obama.

Fifty-four years after laws provided for an adequate education for all, Randolph claimed African-American students were still suing just to receive minimum services. Schools built over 100 years before, he said, had no heat, and when it rained raw sewage flowed down the corridors. Inequities in health care meant that the life expectancy of a black person in South Carolina was six years less than that of whites. In 2008, he told the crowd, black employees in the state government were still paid less than their white colleagues.

With Barack Obama, John Edwards and Hillary Clinton sitting on the podium behind him, Randolph urged the mostly black audience to get out and vote if they wanted to change any of this. He didn't say who he would be supporting, but he did not have to. With a bellowing voice, and fist raised towards the sun, he made his point. "The same hands that used to pick cotton in South Carolina will have the opportunity to pick the next president of the United States," Randolph roared. The crowd went wild.

On the dais, Hillary Clinton wrapped her duffel coat and woollen scarf tightly around her and smiled. She must have lamented how in the space of two weeks she had lost an entire race of people to her young opponent. Days later, South Carolina gave Barack Obama one of the most significant victories of his entire campaign. From then on he could count on the votes of nine out of every ten black Americans. "She was expected to get thirty to forty per cent of the black vote as a result of their legacy," said Max Brantley, referring to how the good feeling towards Bill Clinton at the start of the race should have carried over to Hillary. "By the time it was over, by the time Obama was through with them, they got almost none."

Both Clintons had played some part in the South Carolina loss, and others feel that the Obama campaign deliberately targeted Bill Clinton's strength with African-Americans. But something way beyond their control had happened. The similarities between Dr Martin Luther King and Senator Barack Obama were too obvious to miss. Hope and quiet desperation, plus what both men called "the fierce urgency of now", were building within those who heard the message. While King and Obama may have been more about words than deeds, what they clearly shared was the ability to inspire people – the power to awaken them from their long political sleep.

3

Who's the Most Irish
of Them All?

"I have never had a president who inspired me the way people tell me my father inspired them. But, for the first time, I believe I have found the man who could be that president ..."
– CAROLINE KENNEDY, ENDORSING OBAMA

STELLA O'LEARY OPENED A drawer in her living room where she had shoved the framed photograph soon after hearing the news. There were three people in the picture. On the left, Stella herself was wearing a black furry winter hat, a beaming Hillary Clinton was in the centre, and on the right was Representative Patrick Murphy from Pennsylvania, the second youngest congressman in America and a veteran of the Iraq war. Murphy had the look of a very young Bill Clinton about him. It was the look of someone who was going places.

"He's going in the trash," O'Leary announced, explaining that the dapper Pennsylvanian had delivered the most hurtful betrayal of Hillary by becoming one of the first former Clintonites to endorse Barack Obama for president. "We had worked so hard for him," she sighed, looking at the picture taken on a chilly 2006 autumn day when she and Hillary Clinton had canvassed for Murphy to aid him on his way to Washington. "We organized a huge event up in Philadelphia. We really thought we had a relationship."

Dubliner Stella O'Leary lives and breathes Washington politics. She radiates a natural energy and, from behind round glasses, her deep brown eyes assess the state of play. She speaks with an accent that retains broad Irish tones, sanded down at the edges but preserved through decades of resisting the urge to become truly American. Politics was not in Stella's blood when she arrived in Washington in 1962 to archive a collection of Irish literature at the Catholic University of America. But in 1996, when a group of Irish-Americans decided to help President Clinton with his re-election to a second term, O'Leary entered the fray. "I called the Federal Elections Commission. They said to come down. You signed your name on a piece of paper, and they said, 'Go do whatever you like'."

With permission to fundraise limited amounts of cash to support candidates for local and national elections, O'Leary set up the Irish-American Democrats – a political action committee or "PAC". Carefully placed throughout her home in Bethesda, Maryland, is evidence of a dozen years dedicated to helping the Clintons fulfil their electoral ambitions. There are photos taken with Bill Clinton, and on occasional visits to Stella's I have had the First Lady staring at me from a portrait outside the bathroom door. "She's very serious, earnest, dedicated to politics and extremely knowledgeable," said Stella, confirming that the Hillary Clinton she knows has never bothered with knitting or golf for relaxation. Foreign travel, Stella suspects, has been Clinton's only indulgence, and even it has been "wound into politics".

As one member of a powerful core of Irish-American supporters initially rooting for Hillary Clinton in 2008, O'Leary knew the election was going to be a challenge as soon as she started putting out calls to her regular contacts. "I would approach some people who were contributors or activists and discover they were for Obama." These included Irish-American lawyers and business people on both coasts who were in the habit of writing cheques for the maximum contributions. "My brother was another," she laughed, adding that Democrats who were attracted to Obama early on came from a wide spectrum.

In New York, a key member of the Irish-American lobby had been tilling the ground for Hillary Clinton well before she announced her candidacy. Niall O'Dowd, editor and publisher of *The Irish Voice*, had first met the Clintons seventeen years earlier. In Little Rock, Arkansas, O'Dowd sought out then Governor Bill Clinton, who was exploring a run for the presidency in 1992. Word had spread that the southerner was interested in Northern Ireland, and O'Dowd and others had a hunch that it would be worth making contact with him. The following year, Niall O'Dowd was introduced to Hillary. As American involvement in the peace process grew, the journalist's contacts with the Clinton White House became part of the glue that sealed one of the most productive Irish-American friendships ever.

Like others who have had personal contact with Hillary Clinton, O'Dowd confirmed that, talent and ambition aside, Clinton is defined by her single-minded dedication to whatever she turns her hand to. "What was amazing to me was the transition from First Lady to politician. As a First Lady she was very awkward, standoffish, almost had a kind of a Mary Robinson aura – serene but sort of removed." Sheer perseverance, O'Dowd believed, transformed Clinton into the tireless stump campaigner she had to become to make it to the Senate and then run for the presidency.

No two people agree on Hillary Clinton. Where one person sees a dogged fighter dedicated to social and justice issues, another sees a ruthlessly ambitious woman – feeding into the widely held image of Clinton as a polarising figure. "She's got that reputation of being someone you don't want to confront in the dark," David Keane of the Conservative League of America commented to me early on in the electoral process, alluding to the numerous battles Clinton had waged and won during her White House years with staff, the media and Republicans. From the start of the race, Keane felt she would prove "too hard-edged for most people".

Former Clinton campaign insider Patrick Lewis conceded that she's no "glad hander", but said Hillary herself believed she would win in 2008 by being "supremely competent". By knowing more than any other candidate about the issues facing America, Clinton thought she would edge out the competition.

Niall O'Dowd had witnessed Clinton's "supreme competence" well before her presidential run. "We were in the kitchen of New York's Plaza Hotel with chefs banging pots and pans all around us," he said, recalling an Irish event at which he had asked her to speak. As staff prepared food behind them, O'Dowd quickly tutored her on a range of issues affecting Ireland, North and South. "She just inhaled the briefing, went back upstairs and gave a tremendous press conference."

Knowing these strengths and her commitment to Ireland, *The Irish Voice* never considered supporting any other candidate for the Democratic nomination. The weekly paper, which is distributed in large Irish population centres, urged her to run on the basis that a second President Clinton would be a bonanza for Ireland. "The access Ireland Inc. would have had would have been extraordinary," said O'Dowd, who felt Hillary Clinton had a greater familiarity with Ireland than any candidate who had ever run for the American presidency. In January 2008 the paper endorsed Clinton, claiming "she was with her husband every step of the way during his intervention in the Irish peace process". Barack Obama, the *Voice* commented, had shown a commitment to immigration reform, but "It would be impossible for him to match the sterling record of Hillary Clinton on Irish issues".

While campaign managers fretted over how to keep Bill Clinton occupied, Irish supporters and personal acquaintances, like Declan Kelly, were working with him on the fundraising front. Kelly is one of New York's more recent Irish success stories. From his beginnings as an Irish journalist, Declan Kelly moved into public relations, eventually joining Financial Dynamics, an international network of communications companies stretching from Colombia to Hong Kong. While still in his early thirties, Kelly arrived in Manhattan to oversee the network's US operation and became chairman and CEO for the Americas.

Having met the Irish who make things happen in the Big Apple, Kelly began fundraising for Hillary Clinton's 2006 Senate re-election campaign "in a very minor way". By the time talk of the presidency surfaced, he counted the Clintons among his friends and was approached to help with the financial end of the campaign. "It's very hard to ask people for money but you get used to it after a while," said Kelly, who raised almost $4 million for the effort to get Hillary Clinton elected as America's forty-fourth president. "If you believe in it enough, you do it."

In late 2007 Bill Clinton suggested to Kelly that they add an Irish fundraiser to a trip the former president was taking to London. Using his Irish contacts, Kelly coordinated an event hosted by American-born solicitor Brian Farren and his wife Linda at their Dublin home. Back in 2004 a small-scale event had been held to benefit John Kerry's presidential bid, but at €1,600 a ticket – the maximum allowable individual contribution for the primary election, the Farren's November 2007 event was the largest fundraiser ever held in Ireland for a presidential candidate. So long as the contributions came from Americans or green card holders, there was nothing to stop Irish citizens from accepting invitations to meet Bill. While Hillary Clinton remained on the campaign trail, Bill Clinton flew into Dublin, where he spent two hours in the company of 130 guests, collecting over $300,000 for the campaign war chest.

Back in the US, Irish actor Gabriel Byrne had also been pressed into action on Clinton's behalf. He opened his house in Brooklyn Heights to a Who's Who of Irish-Americans, many from the entertainment and acting world. Declan Kelly and New York hotelier John Fitzpatrick also persuaded the well-heeled in Chicago, Baltimore and California to maximise contributions to fight the looming primary contest and to amass funds for the general election expected to start in February 2008 – by which time Clinton hoped to have clinched the Democratic nomination.

House parties, hosted by friends or influential supporters, were a staple of the Clinton fundraising machine. Early on, top notch functions featured an appearance by either Bill or Hillary. Contributors came away with at least a photograph with one or both of the Clintons and, of course, a peek at a multi-million dollar host home. "The larger donors sat inside the house and the $1,000 contributors were entertained out in the garden," was how one of these private soirees in Maryland was described to me afterwards. The more money you donated, the better chance you had of using a real toilet rather than a port-a-loo in the yard.

Up to 2008, only a tiny percentage of Americans gave money to election campaigns. According to the Center for Responsive Politics in Washington, the figure rarely went over 4 per cent. With a year to go, the 2008 election was already being dubbed the first "billion dollar election", and it would end up costing over two billion dollars. The reasons people donate, according to CRP spokesman Massie Ritsch, are hard to pinpoint. "They may just like the candidates personally, but in our research of almost twenty-five years, we have seen a pattern where contributors do want to support a candidate who is best for their economic self-interest."

In the case of Irish-America, the economic well-being of the "old country" had been a perennial factor for decades. Early on in the 2008 campaign, Barack Obama made it clear that he intended to bring American jobs and profits back to the United States from overseas. One way to do this would be to target "transfer pricing", where, for example, an American company's Irish subsidiary makes a large profit because it is taxed at the low rate of 12.5 per cent in Dublin – while in the US the parent company declares a loss to avoid a much higher American tax. Fear of an assault on American firms doing business in Ireland was another reason why Irish-American Democrats with close ties to home remained within the Clinton camp in the early months of 2008. "That would be disastrous for Ireland," said

O'Dowd. "That's the reason most of the corporations are there – so they can take advantage of Ireland's lenient tax rate."

But despite the astonishing success that Kelly, O'Dowd, O'Leary, Fitzpatrick and Hillary Clinton's other Irish backers had in bringing Irish-American financial muscle to bear, something else was stirring under the radar. Barack Obama was using the internet to generate small amounts of cash from large numbers of people. As the weeks clicked by, Obama's fundraising prowess quickly pushed the amount that each candidate would need to make it through the primaries from an original estimate of $100 million to well over $200 million. As winter gave way to spring, the target figure just kept growing.

Back as far as October 2007, when Hillary Clinton was still comfortably ahead in the polls, there had been ominous warning signs for her. Obama had collected $80 million in campaign contributions, just shy of her $90 million. While she had years of experience and long donor lists to work from, Obama had moved beyond the traditional telephone and contacts book, opting instead for the "pay and click" method of election financing. Following the lead set in 2004 by the early Democratic front-runner Howard Dean, Obama perfected the use of the internet as a means of rapidly raising campaign cash. By the end of January 2008, not only was he a serious political threat to Hillary, but he was beating her in the money stakes, raising $36 million that month to her $14 million. "They got the internet strategy right," said Declan Kelly, marvelling now at how Clinton had managed to keep parity with Obama for so long, given her more plodding methods of collecting contributions.

But it was more than a bunch of tech guys making it happen for Obama. The candidate himself pitched tailored messages to low-income supporters in previously untapped contributor markets. If people could afford only $20 or $30, that's what he asked them for – and it paid off. The Clinton campaign delivered one message to all potential donors, no matter what their income bracket. "You can have Bill Gates manning your internet strategy, but it won't make any difference if you don't have the right candidate," said Kelly, explaining that it was Barack Obama himself who made the difference when it came to internet fundraising.

By the end of January 2008, the country's most prominent Irish-American took the same turn as Patrick Murphy, the congressman whose photograph was headed for Stella O'Leary's dustbin. Ted Kennedy endorsed Barack Obama for president. "I feel change in the air," Kennedy announced to an auditorium packed with students at the Catholic University of America in Washington DC. The senator was flanked by his son Congressman Patrick Kennedy, and his niece Caroline Kennedy. That weekend Caroline had made her feelings clear when she described Obama as "a president like my father". Writing in *The New York Times* she said, "I have never had a president who inspired me the way people tell me my father inspired them. But, for the first time, I believe I have found the man who could be that president – not just for me but for a new generation of Americans."

A political endorsement was a highly unusual move for Caroline Kennedy, who so many older Americans still remembered as a young child at her father's funeral. Though one of the most influential members of the Kennedy clan, Caroline did not involve herself publicly in the family business, preferring the more private world of charities and foundations. Now JFK's only living child was publicly joining forces with his last surviving brother, and it seemed that they were trying to pass something of the Kennedy legacy to a younger generation. Caroline claimed that her teenaged children had first turned her on to Barack Obama.

"A leader who truly has the power to make America good again," was how Ted Kennedy described the young black man beside him, while Obama stood there as coolly as if he had always known where his life's trajectory would take him. It was not the first time a Kennedy had praised Obama. At the funeral of Dr King's wife Coretta Scott King in 2006, Ethel Kennedy – the widow of Robert F. Kennedy – reportedly told Obama, "The torch is being passed to you".

BUT TO SUPPOSE THAT ALL Irish-Americans are Democrats because they hung pictures of John F. Kennedy alongside the Pope in the 1960s is to misunderstand the 35 million people in the United States who call themselves Irish. You had only to watch John McCain speak after his Republican primary victories in New Hampshire, South Carolina or Florida to see the signs that read "Irish for McCain". Everywhere your eye fell another one popped up. Even on the deck of an aircraft carrier near Charleston, South Carolina, McCain's Irish army was at the ready.

"For the first 500 signs we used a small printer in Concord, New Hampshire," explained Jeff Cleary, who started the ball rolling with the placards. The executive director of the Irish-American Republicans handed them out at the early primaries, then printed more up in his home state of New York and mailed them to IAR chapter presidents around the country.

"He absolutely ate it up," said Cleary, describing McCain's reaction to having Irish-American backing. On the aircraft carrier, when the television technicians asked Irish supporters to put down the signs because they were blocking sight of the candidate, McCain directed them to put the signs back up. "It always gave him a chance to tell that hokey Irish joke he loves."

A guy sits down beside another guy in a bar in New York. And he says to him, "Where are you from?"

"I'm from Ireland."

"Really? I'm from Ireland too."

"Great, let me buy you a drink. Whereabouts in Ireland are you from?"

"Dublin."

"I'm from Dublin too. Where did you go to school?"

"I went to St Mary's."

"Wow! I went to St Mary's too. When did you come to America?"

"1970."

"I don't believe it. I came here in 1970 too."

And then another guy walks in and says to the bartender, "What's going on there?"

"Oh, it's just the O'Reilly twins getting drunk again."

McCain's favourite joke didn't cause him any problems until later in the campaign when the Ancient Order of Hibernians in Scranton, Pennsylvania, accused the candidate of engaging in negative stereotyping of the Irish.

John McCain traces his roots back to Antrim and Donegal, and according to Irish-American Republicans chairman Grant Lally, the Senator's work on immigration reform and the peace process gave him sufficient Irish street credibility to match any of the candidates in the 2008 race. "I question Obama's interest or commitment to Ireland or the peace process. He has never indicated any particular support for Ireland," commented Lally.

Back in 1996, however, McCain had opposed giving Gerry Adams a visa to enter America, arguing that it would damage relations with Britain. Again, in 2005, when the McCartney sisters came to Washington seeking justice for the killing of their brother Robert, the Senator maintained a belligerent stance against the IRA and Sinn Féin. Addressing an Ireland Fund dinner during St Patrick's week festivities, John McCain fixed his gaze on Sinn Féin leader Gerry Adams and proclaimed, "There is nothing Republican about the Irish Republican Army."

As a New York attorney, Grant Lally sees today's Irish-America as having become more Republican, particularly since the 1970s. The switch, he believes, is owing to the phenomenon of suburbanisation. "Today it's not widely appreciated, but New York City is virtually devoid of Irish-Americans. The latest number was that either three or four per cent of New York City is of Irish descent. By contrast, the suburbs around New York City are heavily Irish. Nassau County is twenty-five per cent Irish, Suffolk County and Westchester the same," he said.

It is known that people become settled once they migrate to the suburbs, and in the 2000 and 2004 presidential elections that trend translated into more votes for George W. Bush. "In the suburbs Irish-Americans are homeowners and businessmen and women," Lally explained, claiming the main interest became protecting their assets and educating their children. "It's a separation from the urban machines which dominated Irish politics during the first hundred years of the Irish-American experience in the US."

Jeff Cleary sees party loyalty as something many Irish-Americans still inherit from their fathers and grandfathers. That said, his own grandfather, who arrived from Ireland to New York as a Republican, was not initially welcomed. "He walked into a Republican club and they told him to go up to the Democrats. They didn't want him. After that he wouldn't vote Republican if you put a gun to his head," he said. But Cleary's father switched back to the Republican Party, and Jeff followed him. The Irish-American Republicans have been around since the 1880s, and today, he claims, they have chapters in twenty-nine states and members in all fifty.

As a political consultant who cut his teeth advising former New York Republican governor George Pataki, Jeff Cleary is certain that history predisposes Irish-Americans to conservative values. "They look at their ancestors and what they went through in Ireland," Cleary said, adding that when people understand the importance of freedom, they value a strong national defence and a smaller government. "Irish-Americans are very hard-working people. They want to keep more of their money. They don't want to be told what they can and can't do. They don't want government in their life."

Cleary and Lally both acted as floor managers for George W. Bush during the Florida recount in 2000 and were early backers of John McCain – sticking by him in the summer of 2007 when former New York mayor Rudy Giuliani was the presumed Republican nominee for president. "When everyone was on the Rudy bandwagon, we were with John when it was hot and terrible and he was tanking in the polls," recalled Cleary. Straight talk, they believed, pulled McCain out of the hole, particularly on the thorny issue of illegal immigration. "He understands you are not going to line up a bunch of airplanes and send twelve million people back to their home countries. It's not realistic." Voters, Cleary reckoned, would soon get tired of the "teleprompter answers" they were getting on these topics from Barack Obama.

I reminded Cleary that John McCain often regarded the teleprompter as a form of torture, given his inability early in the campaign to follow a script without repeatedly stumbling. "He speaks off the cuff very well. He doesn't need a lot of notes. When Barack Obama doesn't have the teleprompter, he's not great," Cleary assured me. And there's one more thing – Cleary had little stomach for those soaring speeches of Obama's. On Democratic primary nights, he sat in a New York bar along with Clinton campaign people and waited for Obama to speak.

"Here's the game. Every time Obama says hope or change, we do a shot! 'Hope.' 'Change.' 'Hope.' 'Change.' Keep lining up the shots."

BARACK OBAMA DID NOT PLAY UP his Irish credentials, despite the fact that County Offaly laid claim to him early on. In the autumn of 2007 Canon Stephen Neill, the Church of Ireland rector of Moneygall, discovered that Fulmuth Kearney, who left for America in 1850 as a nineteen-year-old, was Obama's great-great-great-grandfather. Records discovered by a researcher in Utah confirmed that the shoemaker's son had sailed to America on board the *SS Marmion*, settled in Indiana, and that his lineage eventually produced Ann Dunham, Barack Obama's Kansan mother. "I was gobsmacked," said Neill, who was besieged by international media as soon as the link was confirmed, but who received no direct contact from Obama's campaign. "I don't think he wants to get into the Irish corner. He certainly isn't courting the Irish vote. I'm happy the link is real, but he probably sees it as something of no great significance," Neill surmised. Demonstrating that he could recognise an Irish accent, Obama responded to a general question from

ITN's Johnny Irvine in Iowa by informing the reporter that he had ancestors in a village in Ireland and that he was "looking forward to having a pint there".

"This is a man who is comfortable in a lot of places in a lot of different situations," said Carol Wheeler, who worked with the Obama campaign on getting out the Irish-American vote. "Everyone wants to be Irish, right. And then to find out, 'My gosh, I really am,' he's absolutely delighted."

But with no prior involvement in the peace process and a raft of urgent global problems vying for his attention, Ireland was not one of Obama's pet subjects. Nonetheless, both the Clinton and Obama campaigns jousted for ownership of the Northern Ireland issue well into the primaries. On St Patrick's Day in 2008, Hillary Clinton released a position paper on Northern Ireland which was met with pointed dispatches from the Obama campaign accusing her of overstating her role in the peace process. "In President Bill Clinton's own book about his role in Northern Ireland, he did not talk about any particular contribution by Hillary Clinton," Obama's campaign manager David Plouffe contended.

In Boston, Irish-American newspaper publisher Ed Forry saw parallels between Obama's campaign and John F. Kennedy's forty-eight years earlier. "Having lived through that, I got a sense that a similar sort of thing was happening for a generation that's now the age I was then," said Forry, who gave his personal endorsement to Obama early in the primary process, despite lingering doubts about the Illinois senator's readiness for high office.

Forry grew up in Dorchester, a multi-ethnic area south of the city of Boston, and believed that in 2008 so-called Irish issues no longer swayed Irish-American voters to the extent they once did. "There was a shared commonality of interest among Irish-Americans and the Irish up until the Irish Tiger," he said, claiming that things had changed. "We have a general sense that you guys over there are doing pretty well, maybe better than some of our people." While the emotional ties between Ireland and the United States would survive, Forry felt the respective interests had diverged over the last decade. "We part company when we go to Shannon and find that people go out on the tarmac and start beating the crap out of American planes, and that some of our soldiers passing through Shannon to Iraq are being treated shabbily by Irish citizens. We find that to be offensive, even though I don't agree with American policy."

While Ed Forry shares a concern for the undocumented Irish still living in America's shadows, he regards the notion of special immigration deals for the Irish in today's environment as "preposterous". In addition to an Irish newsletter, he publishes a Haitian paper to provide information for immigrants from an island where the average income is only a few dollars a day. I got the impression that Ed Forry felt a more urgent need to assist the Haitians in Boston than the Irish.

Rather than appeal to specific ethnic groups, Barack Obama's campaign sought to promote the candidate's broad appeal. Irish who supported him did so initially as individuals, rather than through coordinated Irish groups – though the campaign would later appoint Carol Wheeler to reach out to Irish-American voters and Trina Vargo would advise on Irish issues. Both women have extensive contacts in the Irish-American world.

Earlier, Barack Obama had tapped Irish-born Harvard academic Samantha Power to be a senior foreign policy adviser to his 2008 campaign. Obama had asked to meet Power after her

Pulitzer prize-winning book *A Problem from Hell*, examining America's failure to act against genocide, caught his attention in 2005. "We were supposed to meet for an hour, and an hour gave way to two hours and three hours and four hours," Power told RTÉ in March 2008. She was so impressed by the freshman senator that she took leave of absence from her position at Boston's Harvard University to go to Washington to work for him. "I heard myself saying, 'Why don't I leave Harvard and come down here and work as an intern in your office?' I would have done anything for this person I was meeting. I couldn't believe that someone of his qualities was willing to be in politics."

Samantha Power, who moved from Dublin to America as a child, became an early casualty of the bitter war of words that developed between Hillary Clinton and Barack Obama as the primary battle heated up. In an off-the-record comment to *The Scotsman* newspaper in March 2008, Power described Clinton as "a monster" who was "stooping to anything" to win. The comments were printed, and in the heat of the moment Power stepped down from her role as adviser. She was tipped to rejoin an Obama administration.

As Barack Obama's star hit the stratosphere in the winter of 2008, Stella O'Leary was aware of dissatisfaction in the Clinton camp that he could not be stopped at an early stage of the game. "There was a major irritation that he was in the race at all," she said, referring to feedback from meetings Stella had with members of Clinton's Capitol Hill staff during the early primaries. "He had a kind of brash self-confidence about him that was a surprise. Mostly it was anger at him being here and taking from the presumptive nominee," O'Leary said. "It would be like someone who got elected last year having taken over from Bertie," said Caitríona Fitzpatrick, who was privy to meetings with key advisers inside the Clinton campaign. "You think, sure he's only being backed by university students, and he's just being a bit rebellious. But is he really a serious contender? People didn't think he was."

Internal war was simmering a level higher up among the core Clinton campaign team. This included Mark Penn, the sometimes gruff but brilliant election strategist, long-time Clinton confidant Harold Ickes, media man Howard Wolfson and campaign manager Patti Solis Doyle. "Penn was keeping her away from the press and keeping Chelsea out of it," said O'Leary, referring to the bubble that Clinton was confined to in the run-up to the Iowa caucus. "This business of protecting her was crazy."

Despite public perception of Hillary Clinton as a polarising figure and her problematic 2002 vote for the Iraq war, Clinton's Irish supporters believed campaign mismanagement caused her to fall behind at the start. "In the second half she was by far the dominant figure and ran the thing herself," said Declan Kelly, referring to Clinton's string of victories months later when she outpolled Barack Obama by margins of two to one. Niall O'Dowd agreed that Obama deftly rode a wave of "hope" and "change" through the early spring, while Clinton allowed herself to be over-managed to the point that she lost sight of who she was and what she stood for.

"It reminded me of the middle stages of the Gore campaign, when you had this almost manufactured candidate and you couldn't get to the real person," O'Dowd said. "I didn't know Al Gore, but I certainly know Hillary. The real person is a very decent, remarkable human being, and the frustration was not seeing that persona come out until too late in the game."

4

The Outsider

"He was able to move in different worlds, the world of the streets, the world of the foundations, the world of the media who would cover us and the business and government interests we would deal with." – OBAMA SUPPORTER JERRY KELLMAN

A T TWENTY-THREE BARACK OBAMA started his working life as a community organiser. After graduating from Columbia University, he took a job, briefly, at a New York financial company before sending his résumé to Jerry Kellman in Chicago. Working with local churches, Kellman was putting together community initiatives to boost Chicago's economically depressed South Side. "In an all black area I felt it was appropriate that we have a black organiser but it was easier said than done, and I was having trouble finding one," Kellman said, recalling his first contact with Barack Obama. "I felt that Barack wanted to be a civil rights organiser, but he was ten or twelve years too young. The civil rights movement was no longer there and this was the closest thing he could find to it."

What Kellman liked about Obama was what many have described as his "otherness". "As an outsider he identified with other people who were outsiders," Kellman said. "He had grown up an American abroad in Asia. He had grown up an African-American in Hawaii at a time when there were very few African-Americans there." Though Obama had better educational and financial opportunities than those he was being recruited to organise, Kellman knew Obama would understand them.

Two decades later, Barack Obama was still connecting with voters by presenting himself as an outsider attempting to conquer the power structure from the fringes. A fresh face and articulate candidate, his brand of politics was to move beyond the divisiveness and negativity associated with Washington, which had turned so many people off government. Obama was only two years on Capitol Hill before he announced his run for president. Though he lacked traditional experience, he claimed he didn't want to give Washington any more time to "boil all the hope" right out of him. This insurgent outsider status appealed to the coalition of African-Americans, students and educated liberals he was building around his campaign.

But each of these blocks was also drawn to Obama for its own reason. Young people identified with his multicultural background and his global view of politics. His tenure as the first African-American editor of the *Harvard Law Review* impressed educated whites who saw a mould-breaker. Black voters valued the time Obama had spent toiling on Chicago's meaner streets. They were all looking at his biography, and it was a most unusual one.

Barack Obama was probably conceived in a college dormitory at the University of Hawaii in Honolulu. His mother, eighteen-year-old anthropology student Ann Dunham, fell in love with Barack Obama senior, the university's first ever African student who came from Kenya in 1959 to get an American education. "My father grew up herding his father's goats and attending the local school set up by the British colonial administration where he had shown great promise," Obama wrote in his 1995 memoir *Dreams from My Father*. Kenya was close to winning independence from Britain, and its top students had been sent abroad so they could bring back knowledge to help the country develop. Much had been expected of Obama senior, the son of a member of Kenya's Luo tribe.

Ann Dunham, a descendant of Fulmuth Kearney from County Offaly, was born in Kansas. In 1960 Dunham moved to Hawaii with her father Stanley, a furniture salesman, and her mother Madelyn, who would work her way up to vice-president of a bank. It not clear if the Dunhams were happy about their daughter's relationship with the Kenyan scholar, but they welcomed him into their home and the students quickly married. In *Dreams from My Father* Obama noted that in 1961, the year his parents married, miscegenation – or inter-racial breeding – was still a crime in over half of America's states. "In many parts my father could have been strung up from a tree for merely looking at my mother the wrong way; in the most sophisticated of northern cities, the hostile stares, the whispers, might have driven a woman in my mother's pre-dicament into a back alley abortion."

On 4 August 1961 Barack Hussein Obama was born in Honolulu. He was given his father's full name. The young Obama has no memories of life with both parents because by the time he was two years old his father was gone. To further his studies, Obama senior accepted a scholarship to Harvard

University in Boston, but there was not enou
his young family with him. He never came b
returned to Kenya where he started a new fan
American woman. There in Africa, Obama se
first wife and two older children whom he hac
tially coming to America.

Young Barack, or "Barry Obama" as he was called as a
child, thus began life as an outsider. As the son of an absent
African father and a mother whose skin, Obama wrote, was
"white as milk", he was already an odd-boy-out on the Pacific
island paradise of Hawaii.

Ann Dunham divorced Barack's father and in 1967 married
another student, this time an Indonesian. Soon after, Indonesia's
ruler Suharto ordered his country's citizens to return home. As a
six-year-old, Obama moved with his mother to Jakarta to live
with the new man in their lives, Lolo Soetoro. "People swirled
about us speaking rapidly in a language I didn't know, smelling
unfamiliar," Obama recalled, describing the chaos of their arrival at Jakarta's airport as Soetoro negotiated his family's entry
with soldiers dressed in brown uniforms.

Though their new home was a far cry from what they had
been used to in Hawaii, Obama wrote that his mother was willing to put up with inconveniences, including dysentery and
fevers, as well as "having to squat over a hole in the ground to
pee". As Obama remembers it, his mother saw the move to Indonesia as a way to help her husband rebuild that country, as
well as a means of escape from her parents. To make Barack
feel welcome, his new stepfather filled the back yard of their
house with all kinds of exotic animals, including a monkey.
Ann, who was determined that her son receive a good educa-

abroad, got Obama up at 4 a.m. for three hours of extra lessons before school.

Where candidates spent their early childhood had previously seldom mattered in presidential politics, but Obama felt his time in Indonesia imparted valuable insights into the world beyond America's shores. "Probably the strongest experience I have in foreign relations is the fact that I spent four years overseas when I was a child in Southeast Asia," he said in November 2007.

Barack Obama might have scored higher points against someone like George W. Bush, who had rarely been outside the US before being elected president in 2000. But Hillary Clinton, who claimed to have visited eighty countries since entering politics, was not inclined to count Obama's Indonesian adventure as foreign policy experience. "Voters will have to judge if living in a foreign country at the age of ten prepares one to face the big complex international challenges the next president will face," Clinton retorted in a televised debate. "I think we need a president with more experience than that!"

Some voters concurred, but others were not sure. There was a growing feeling that Obama's Asian exposure, combined with his African roots, made him the embodiment of global politics that the next president must navigate and thoroughly understand. Knowing how people pee in Indonesia, or having a rudimentary knowledge of goat herding in Africa, gave Obama a familiarity with world cultures which other candidates could not match.

A more contentious aspect of Obama's years in Jakarta was that he had attended a Muslim school for two years, leading to persistent claims in the US that he had been raised a Muslim. In his memoir he noted that in that school the teacher "wrote to tell my mother that I made faces during Koranic verses".

Obama also disclosed that his grandfather in Kenya was a Muslim, his own father an atheist and his mother a "secular humanist". Obama avoided any references to the practice of religion in his younger years, but failure to fully explain any Islamic exposure dogged his campaign throughout.

"He's a Muslim," a good friend insisted when I asked for her thoughts on Obama. She couldn't remember where she had heard it, but she was "pretty sure" it was true – one of many Americans who believed Obama was deliberately hiding his true faith and could not be trusted.

"There were people who bought into these silly emails that said Senator Obama gave his oath of office on the Koran," said Rory Finnin, who canvassed for Obama in several states. "We would do our best to dispel these myths, but some people demonstrated an unwillingness to listen – which I can only explain as a kind of racism."

Even as controversy erupted over Obama's twenty-year membership of Chicago's protestant Trinity United Church and his association with the Reverend Jeremiah Wright, suggestions of a Muslim background failed to subside. At the click of a mouse, the internet produces hundreds of articles claiming that Obama could have been given the Arabic middle name Hussein only by a Muslim father, and the blogosphere is filled with stories that Obama's religion was listed as Islam while in Indonesia.

The Obama campaign returned fire with a dedicated website of its own, FightTheSmears.com, focusing on Obama's Christian faith. But having to repeatedly deny that he had ever been a Muslim was not something a candidate preaching multicultural solutions to international problems relished. Obama found such denials offensive both to Muslims in general and to individuals like Saad Sultan, an Iraqi government official who felt a kinship with Obama because the candidate's grandfather had been an African Muslim. "Every time I see Obama I say, 'He's close to us. Maybe he'll see us in a different way'," Sultan told the *New York Times* on 17 July 2008. Obama would continue to tread a fine line on the issue of religious faith but at the same time courted electoral support from Catholics, Evangelicals and non-Christians alike.

That Barack Obama was not the stereotypical all-American candidate was a problem for voters who like simple homegrown stories. His globetrotting mother was no longer alive (Ann Dunham died of ovarian cancer in 1995 at the age of fifty-two, and his step-grandmother often gave press interviews from her hut in Kenya. He had numerous half-brothers and sisters scattered across the planet, and Obama had spent four years in the world's most populous Muslim nation. It was a web of connections too far removed from American apple pie and the Fourth of July for some Americans to appreciate. Yet others, particularly the younger generation, saw 2008 as a chance to break the outdated biographical mould of the White House hopeful. Obama's family history might not fit the sunny ideal that the older generation still clung to, but it more accurately reflected the diverse reality of the twenty-first century.

When "Barry" was ten, he returned from Indonesia to live with his grandparents in Hawaii. His mother followed with his half-sister Maya who was born abroad. Around the same time Barry's African father paid a visit to Honolulu. Obama senior had been built up in the young boy's mind as a semi-royal figure performing important work in Kenya. But he was perplexed by this tall dark stranger, who scolded him for watching too much television and directed him to study like his half-brothers and sisters in Africa. "I decided I preferred his more distant image, an image I could alter on a whim," Obama wrote years later. That was the last time they saw each other.

Obama's passion was sport and most of his waking hours were spent with a football or a basketball. As a bi-racial teenager, he also grappled with race and identity. The innocence of his childhood had passed – replaced by the weighty reality that he was a black youth being raised by a white family. At Occidental College in Los Angeles Obama found himself drawn to black friends and into heated discussions about race.

"When I knew him, he was just one of my bros," said Eric Moore, who became fast friends with Obama when they met in college. "I asked him, 'So what kind of a name is Barry Obama for a brother?' We kind of chuckled and he said, 'Well, my real name is Barack Obama'. So I said, 'Barack is a very strong name,' and I never called him Barry after that. Everyone called him Barry, but it just didn't sound right to me."

Moore, an African-American, had come from Boulder, Colorado, a mainly white town and, like Obama, his parents had divorced when he was young, leaving him too without a father figure. "I think we both came to LA for a similar reason, which was to get the urban black experience, to help us understand our lives." What they were looking for was not hard to find in Los Angeles, and together Moore and Obama explored what they had been missing. "We'd go and get our hair cut in the hood, in the African-American community, because no one else could cut it," Moore said. "I had a car. We'd go to concerts and festivals. We sought out all the culture and music available. That's what you get in a big city. That's what he was looking for."

To Eric Moore, Obama seemed very polished for a seventeen-year-old. "He carried himself in a very dignified way, not cocky, just a very confident comfortable young man. What I concluded later was that his background probably had a lot do with establishing his personality and demeanour." Eric Moore also heard the first public speech that Barack Obama delivered, which was at a Black Student Alliance rally on the college campus. Like many in the late 1970s, students in LA were up in arms about apartheid and demanding that college authorities cancel any investments in South Africa. "His voice boomed out of an unlikely body," said Moore, who recalled how the "skinny kid" commanded the attention of students and faculty, even though Obama was new to the campus.

Eric Moore and Barack Obama never talked about what career paths they might follow, and after two years they went their separate ways. Moore remained in Los Angeles where he settled into corporate real estate, but some years ago he spotted an Obama election volunteer in Chicago and reconnected with his old college friend. During the 2008 presidential campaign he only saw Obama for "a few minutes" here and there at campaign events.

I was curious to know if Barack Obama – the politician – was the same man Eric Moore had known at Occidental College thirty years before. "He's the same guy," Moore replied without hesitation. "It's funny because everything he says is exactly the way I think, his perspective on the world and politics. We took the same classes, we had the same professors. We are sort of cut from the same cloth in terms of our life perspective, so I can really connect with the things he says."

THE TIP OF CHICAGO WHICH BORDERS the state of Indiana used to be one of the world's largest steel-producing areas. By the mid-1980s, however, it was in a rut. Plants had shut down, and economic devastation had come to working-class and African-American neighbourhoods. "We could not make the workers understand that those plants and those jobs were not going to open back up," said Loretta Augustine-Herron, a black community worker who lived in the middle of the threatened area. It was the same spot where twenty-three-year-old Barack Obama had landed in his continuing quest to find his place in the world. "He figured the black community in Chicago would be exciting, a vibrant place that he could belong to," said Mike Kruglik, who met Obama when he arrived in the city. "When he got there, he found out he was going to have to recreate the community in order to have one to belong to."

Listening to Jerry Kellman run through the job description of community organising he gave to Barack Obama back in 1985, you begin to wonder if the White House might be less demanding. Obama's task was to form relationships with people in the community by interviewing them and listening to their stories. He needed to challenge them to get involved with one another to tackle issues they cared about. To do this, he would have to teach poorly educated people how to confront a major corporation or government body, how to negotiate and how to deal with the media. "This meant learning it himself before he could teach them," Kellman explained, adding that Obama was expected to develop an "institutional base of organisations" to support the effort.

"Gee, he's awfully young," was Loretta Augustine-Herron's first reaction when she met Obama at a church hall near the Altgeld Gardens housing complex, a home to 2,000 people. But she conceded that Obama quickly turned their problems into issues for which they could fight. "We didn't know the difference between a problem and an issue, but he taught us that. He helped us identify the city or state agency that took care of it," she recalled.

Organising was a seven-day-a-week job. Most of the work was done through faith-based groups, so Obama usually spent his Sundays at churches. "He was pretty stretched out," said Loretta, who maintained that she has never met someone so young who was quite so disciplined in both his work and personal habits. "He'd just stick to salads because he said heavy meals weighed him down and prevented him from thinking clearly," she said, laughing at how he would pick at food.

Like all efforts at large-scale change, the results proved disappointing. Linda Randle, who campaigned with Obama to have asbestos removed from the Altgeld Gardens and Ida B. Wells public housing projects, remembers the day she and Barack Obama took a group to discuss the problem with the Chicago Housing Authority.

"We were supposed to have a meeting with the director at ten that morning. So Barack got on the bus coming from Altgeld, and I had my people get on the bus from Ida B. Wells," Linda explained. "By one o'clock, we were still sitting there waiting for this meeting to happen. So we called the media to come over and be with us. Someone whispered to the director's assistant that the media were in there with us. So they said, 'Would you all like coffee?' We said, 'No. We want this meeting to go on.' So we sat there for another two or three hours."

By that evening buses had come to pick them up and everyone left without the meeting taking place. Despite the snub and the five-hour wait, Randle said Barack Obama would not let them get angry. "He says anger was a waste of time, didn't do anything but raise your blood pressure." Obama would carry his calm demeanour into political life. His refusal to lose his cool, even when provoked by testy opponents or backhanded tactics, became legendary. On the 2008 presidential trail campaign staff took to calling him "No Drama Obama".

Not long into his job as an organiser, Barack Obama learned that his community volunteers were quitting. "We weren't empowered. It just didn't seem like we were making any headway," said Loretta Augustine-Herron, recalling her frustration at dealing with city authorities. Obama remembered it too, and in 2008 he told voters at campaign rallies how he had looked out the window of that meeting room and seen kids throwing stones aimlessly up at an abandoned building. He asked Loretta and the others what would happen if they all just walked away and gave up. "He let us have it," said Loretta. "He kind of shamed us and we probably needed it at the time. He got us back."

Jerry Kellman was surprised that Obama lasted as long as he did on the job. "Most people get burnt out. I always turned around to see if he was still there." If he had stuck with it, Kellman believes Obama would have been the best community organiser in America. But after four years of trying to effect change "from the bottom up", Obama told fellow organiser Mike Kruglik that he was going to Harvard Law School. He planned to learn about "how powerful people think, particularly people that make laws and economic decisions, people who control the flow of money". Kruglik was not convinced that college would teach Obama about ordinary people becoming powerful. "I suggested that he might learn more by continuing to do it than by going off to Harvard," he said. But Obama's mind was made up.

Kellman, who had opened up the world of community organising to Obama, knew that the ambitious youngster would move on. "He was going back and forth on the two challenges that his mother had presented to him as he was growing up. The first being 'achievement' and the second 'service'. The organising was obviously the service part. It didn't do much for him in terms of achievement," said Kellman.

Another event that may have influenced Obama's direction was his first trip to Kenya. In 1982 Obama senior had died in a car crash, prompting Obama to explore his African roots and connect with his family there. "He talked about his father when he told me he was leaving organising," Kellman told me, noting that Obama had got to know something of his father's story once his half-sister and brother came to America. The impression Obama received was that the old man had been overly idealistic, had fallen on the wrong side of Kenyan politics and had ended up destitute. "That was of concern to Barack," said Kellman, who believed Obama had reached a point where he feared the same thing could happen to him. "He was always interested in beginning a family, although he hadn't met the right girl yet. He didn't see organising as a stable way to do that. He was scared if he was not practical that he could end up like his father who had been very idealistic, achieving nothing and disappointing those who depended on him."

"If he can do it, so can I!" intoned Loretta Augustine-Herron, explaining how Barack Obama inspired her to go back to college after he left for Harvard. She earned her Bachelor's and Master's degrees and became a special education teacher. In 2007 the school near Altgeld Gardens where Loretta was teaching closed because enrolment had fallen from 1,200 students to 260. As Barack Obama fought his way to the White House, the dreary housing complex where he learned about life on the bottom rung was being renovated and was largely empty.

Jerry Kellman left organising, too, for divinity school. When you ask Kellman what made Obama stand out, there is a familiar ring to his response. Barack Obama in his twenties, it seemed, was just a less polished version of the man who rose to become one of America's greatest political sensations.

"He was able to move in different worlds, the world of the streets, the world of the foundations, the world of the media who would cover us and the business and government interests we would deal with," said Kellman. "He was very committed, and when he encountered difficulty or frustration, he was capable of using his own resources to regroup, learn from the experience and start again. He had a good sense for strategy. He learned quickly and was always hungry to learn."

THE PROCESS OF MOVING IN THESE different worlds gave Obama an edge over his classmates when in 1989 he arrived at Harvard Law School. At twenty-seven he was older than many of the other students, who had come directly from elite schools without ever having worked. Barack Obama had a firm grasp of arguments and through extensive reading had discovered an access route to the world of intellectual ideas.

Boston's Harvard Law School is a bastion of liberalism and its mouthpiece is the *Harvard Law Review*. Written, edited and published by the students themselves, it has long been a showcase for student research and writing. The *Law Review* is widely read among the American legal profession, and by the end of his first year Obama was contributing articles and later became its editor. He may have already been considering a future in electoral politics by the time classmates urged him to run for president of the *Law Review*. "He did tell me he had possible thought of becoming mayor [of Chicago]," said Mike Kruglik.

Though being president of the *Law Review* was not necessarily part of that plan he did submit his name. When the school's vote developed into a battle for control of the *Review*'s message between the dominant liberals and a growing conservative bloc, Obama emerged as a consensus candidate who could work with both sides. By the time the shouting was done, the former community organiser had won his first election.

As the only African-American to have held the position up to then, Obama drew national attention. Job offers poured in from top law firms, complete with promises of fast-track positions and six-figure salaries. "We'll add your name to the list," was reportedly what staff at Harvard told firms seeking to recruit the black wonder. He was also offered a clerkship with a federal judge, another expeditious path to the top of the legal profession.

But Barack Obama was not interested in moving to the inside without using his status to speak for those who could not speak for themselves. He had come to Harvard to learn how ordinary people could become influential. Now that he had learned the theories behind power and achieved a measure of it along the way, he was setting his sights on the city of Chicago once again. Obama was thirty-one. In sixteen years he would be on his way to the White House.

5

Hillary's Sniper Fire

"So I made a mistake. It proves I'm human."
– HILLARY CLINTON

"**W**HAT IS EVERYONE CHEERING FOR?" shouted the Chicago teacher, trying to massage her daughter's shoulders while they stood in the middle of the heaving crowd. "Georgia," a young man in an Obama t-shirt replied, pointing to a map of America on big television screens erected beside the stage. "So, he has Illinois and Georgia, and she has Oklahoma, Tennessee and New Jersey," the schoolteacher said. "Oh, that's not good." The crowd tilted towards the screen again to hear the prediction that Hillary Clinton would win another state. A "booing" sound rose up around the room.

The Obama supporters and volunteers – crammed into the ballroom of a downtown Chicago hotel – were hot, exhausted and hungry, but in the "Yes we can!" spirit of the campaign they had taken this far, they were not about to flunk out on Super Tuesday. With half the total number of delegates required to secure both Democratic and Republican nominations at stake, and twenty-two states holding their primary elections, 5 February 2008 was dubbed "Tsunami Tuesday".

Hours earlier I had joined the crowd in the ballroom, which had been cleared by Secret Service personnel assigned to protect Barack Obama. At events where the candidate was due to appear, the drill was to assign journalists to their own section. "Media Access Only" sounded great, except that once you arrived it was often a letdown. Members of the press were routinely herded into a pen at the very back of the hall, with little access to the ordinary supporters, and positioned as far away from the candidate as possible.

Tonight I had decided to ditch my press credentials and my radio microphone. Instead, I joined the line of invited guests. Invitations to see Barack Obama on Super Tuesday had been offered to his supporters over the internet and snapped up like rock concert tickets. I did not have one, but a woman standing in the queue agreed to take me in as her guest. Together we cruised by the Secret Service agent, who shook my Mini Disc recorder a few times before handing it back to me. I was now a citizen journalist masquerading as an Obama supporter. I would do the same with all the candidates.

Inside, members of the campaign staff selected "faces" to position behind Obama during his televised address. The main criterion was that they be youthful – with an equal spread of black, brown and white faces preferred. Not wishing to be that conspicuous, I staked out a spot in front of the stage where Obama would speak. I was joined by hundreds of local African-Americans, students and Democratic politicians all of whom had spent a long day urging people to the polls in rain-drenched Chicago.

"I'm so tired I can feel a heartbeat in my feet," declared an elderly black woman, who moved through the crowd selling "Obama for President" pins. She had boarded a bus at 4 a.m. in Grand Rapids, Michigan, 180 miles northeast of Chicago. By nine that morning she was making phone calls and handing out flyers for Obama in downtown Chicago, and by 9 p.m. this ambitious grandmother was fundraising by selling election paraphernalia. I pointed to an unusual badge with a sapling taking root underneath an American flag, and before I knew it, she had pinned it on my chest. "Next we'll be working on going to the convention, because he's going to win," the woman said, fleecing me of six dollars. "Oh, yes he is!" she repeated happily and sidled over to her next customer. With volunteers like that, it was easy to see how Barack Obama had made such extraordinary progress.

"Take a look at this map," said a television pundit, who pointed to Massachusetts and predicted a Clinton victory there. "No she can't! No she can't!" the tired crowd began. But before they could work it up to a full chant, Obama added Delaware and Connecticut to his tally, as well as Alabama in the deep south, and the chanting switched to "Yes we can!"

This familiar rallying cry had been snatched from Obama's 2004 Senate campaign. At first Obama hated it, and believed it didn't mean anything – but it stuck. Then a cast of musical artists and Hollywood stars made a campaign anthem out of "Yes we can!" by setting one of Obama's speeches to music. The hit song was the start of what opponents deemed to be the "cult of celebrity" surrounding Barack Obama. That night in Chicago, the music was a calming influence on the nervous crowd.

In a tit-for-tat result pattern, the next state Hillary Clinton won was Arkansas, where Bill Clinton had served as governor before becoming president in 1992. Then Obama evened up the score by taking Louisiana. "Oh my God! This is the most excited, this is the most inspired, this is the most engaged I've ever been in my entire life!" a young black girl shrieked into my recorder. Tina was from an impoverished part of Chicago, and until she began volunteering for Barack Obama she never thought she would care a damn about politics. For the first time, Tina was learning about civics, making new friends and hanging out in a fancy downtown hotel where she was not the hired help. "I'm just so grateful to be a part of it. I'm praying with all my being that he wins," she told me.

To prepare us for Obama's arrival, the floor managers shut off the television screens and turned up a recording of U2 singing "Beautiful Day". The only problem was that over in New York Hillary Clinton had begun speaking. Had it been beautiful over there too, or was she in the dumps for having failed to sweep the board? We weren't going to know. We were in "Obamaland", where the apparent strategy was to switch off the opposition. In truth, Super Tuesday had not given either candidate enough votes, states or delegates to close the deal. It was open to each to spin it as they pleased. And that's what Barack Obama did when, from behind a red velvet curtain, he took his place before the rows of carefully chosen faces.

"There is one thing that we do not need the final results to know," Obama announced. "Our time has come."

At six foot two, Barack Obama dominates almost any setting. His shirts are always white. His suits are pressed and dark. He moves quickly along the front of a crowd, using both hands to efficiently touch as many palms as possible. Supporters with the highest reach have the best chance of making contact, though it is not so much a firm handshake as a quick finger grab. There's no time for words as security men keep him moving up the line. Although he must have been touching hundreds of supporters every day, Obama looked to be sa- vouring the experience that night in Chicago. Despite the rig- ours of the campaign, he appeared younger than his forty-six years, almost too young to be president.

"Yes we can! Yes we can! Yes we can!" Our ballroom sim- ply erupted before him.

Having come to this event as a guest, I now found myself in the middle of the mania as I swayed with a throng of Obama supporters, all eager for their fix of the man and the message that had driven them to become his street and cyber- prophets. Straining to maintain my footing, I held aloft my radio recorder as candidate and crowd fed off one another. Each time Obama tossed them a smart new line, they recipro- cated with thankful cheers and spurred him to even greater oratorical heights. All of them were players in a symphony of mutual recognition.

Near her husband, Michelle Obama stood tall in a red de- signer outfit with puffed sleeves, more like a First Lady-in- waiting than a candidate's wife with many rounds still to fight. Standing just feet from the Obamas, I caught that same glimpse of imminent victory that I had seen back at the Jefferson Jack- son dinner in Iowa the previous November – the distinct aura of promise that surrounds the two of them when they are to- gether, like a preview of an upcoming show that you do not want to miss.

Now locked in a serious battle with the Clintons, the time for courteous compliments between the two camps was over. "You have a choice between a candidate who takes more money from Washington lobbyists than do the Republicans, and a candidate who has not taken a dime of their money because we have been funded by *you*," Obama told us. "Fired up! Ready to go!" came the response. Then Barack Obama turned to the bread-and-butter issues that worried every American as the economy slid toward recession.

"You are tired of watching while another family puts up a 'For Sale' sign in their yard," he said. "Tired of seeing another young soldier leave on a tour of duty for a war that should never have been authorised. Maybe this year we don't have to settle for politics where scoring points is more important than solving problems."

Obama's rejection of petty political bickering was at the core of his appeal to Democratic primary voters. But right up to November 2008, the presidential election was dominated by the very slash-and-burn politics he rejected. It demonstrated that simply wanting things to change was not enough to make it happen.

After an exhausting year on the road since announcing his candidacy, Barack Obama knew that a deadlocked contest meant several more months of campaigning if he was to win the Democratic nomination. If anyone in the Chicago crowd that night was thinking of quitting, the Illinois senator brought them back to the first community meeting he had organised in 1985, just miles from where he was standing. "We had made phone calls, knocked on doors, put out flyers, but nobody showed up," he said. But Obama had not allowed his volunteers at the housing projects to quit back then, and as a candidate for the White House, he wasn't going let any of them quit now. Only persistent effort, Obama told the crowd, would bring real change. "That's right!" a voice from somewhere rang out across the silence that descended on the hotel ballroom as we listened. I caught Michelle Obama's hand on the rope line afterward. "Time to get some rest," I said, speaking as much for myself as for her. "Alright!" she laughed, knowing there was little chance of rest anytime soon.

ON SUPER TUESDAY THE CLINTON campaign was dealing with a crisis it had failed to predict. The primary race was supposed to be history. "It'll be over by February fifth," Clinton said just weeks before. But when the day arrived, what she found was Obama and his coalition of young people, African-Americans and college-educated whites blocking her way forward and gaining strength.

On the face of it, Super Tuesday was not a total bust for Hillary Clinton, who won the delegate-rich states of New York, New Jersey and California. Near Clinton headquarters in Arlington, Virginia, Caitríona Fitzpatrick celebrated in a bar with other campaign workers as they waited for California – the biggest delegate prize of all – to be called for Clinton. "It was only the next day, when the numbers had been stacked up, that we kind of realised, 'Well, what's next?' All the smaller states – and we didn't even know who was working on them or looking after them – suddenly became hugely significant." Small states that Clinton did not bargain on campaigning in included Virginia, Maryland and the District of Columbia. "We had loads of work to do," said Fitzpatrick.

Worst still, the Clinton campaign was low on funds. In January 2008, Clinton's team had collected $14 million in donations – less than half of Obama's $36 million haul. But the first real sign that the Clinton machine had been hobbled by the freshman Illinois senator came after Super Tuesday, when Clinton lent her election campaign $5 million from her personal fortune.

The mood among some campaign staff had deteriorated too. Mid-level advisers and organisers travelling with Clinton didn't know if they would be working from week to week, and some were already scouting around for other jobs. Animosities over who was to blame for Clinton's loss of a once towering lead spilled over into the press. "Your ad doesn't work!" strategist Mark Penn shouted at Clinton's ad-maker Mandy Grunwald, according to the *Wall Street Journal* of 14 February 2008. Describing a heated argument between the two, the paper reported that Grunwald replied, "Oh, it's always the ad, never the message."

"They could never really figure out who she was," said author Sally Bedell Smith, guessing as to why the team could not agree on a clear image for Hillary Clinton. "Her campaign was such a confusing series of tactics, slogans and even personalities." Many commentators agreed that in trying to reshape her image to answer Obama's challenge, Clinton exhibited multiple personalities. Some days voters saw a vulnerable Hillary, on other days she became sharply mocking, and later she appeared as a beer-chugging populist. Even her own management team were left guessing as to which persona would next appear.

Constant rumours of trouble inside the campaign reminded Bedell Smith of how staff in Clinton White House had operated. "There were a lot of factions who were set against each other back in those years – with duplicate jobs, turf wars and rivalries." To some extent, Bedell Smith believed those same rivalries surfaced again in 2008. "It's largely the same cast of characters," she said, referring to Hillary's top staffers.

With Clinton's White House bid floundering, campaign manager Patti Solis Doyle was replaced by Maggie Williams.

another Clinton loyalist. "It suddenly went from being a ranking system of director, supervisor and intern to 'Everybody works here for the same thing. We are all working equally as hard.' The attitude changed like that. We all attended all the meetings," said Caitríona Fitzpatrick, who was assigned to the "political room" at headquarters. Her job was to drum up new endorsements for Hillary Clinton and to ensure that staff and volunteers in crucial states had everything they required.

Even though he cost the campaign over $3 million a month, Mark Penn – who acted as both pollster and chief strategist – survived the Super Tuesday shake-up. "There was a sense of 'That man was paid a huge amount of money, but we didn't get the result we wanted from him'," Caitríona Fitzpatrick said, when modestly paid staff and unpaid interns like herself discovered what he was charging. Penn was under pressure to quickly come up with a new strategy to match how Obama's team, led by David Axelrod and David Plouffe, was managing its candidate.

RIGHT AFTER SUPER TUESDAY, BARACK OBAMA hit his stride, tapping deeper into the political and cultural phenomenon that he had become. Up and down the country, he filled stadiums to capacity. Even those suspicious of the candidate lined up with eighteen-year-olds at college arenas to glimpse the man who was something of a cross between civil rights leader Martin Luther King and rapper Jay-Z. On the campaign plane Obama listened to hip-hop on his iPod and relaxed by watching sports on ESPN. To keep fit, he played basketball with his personal aide Reggie Love. By February 2008, Barack Obama's confidence as a presidential candidate was soaring.

At each venue I attended, there were three noteworthy things that Obama said and one clever tactic he used to draw in votes. First, he reminded people that he had opposed the Iraq war from the start and would take out troops if elected president. By then three-quarters of Americans believed the decision to invade Iraq had been incorrect. Obama had not yet begun to emphasise his belief that some of these troops would have to be diverted to Afghanistan to quell growing violence there.

Second, Senator Obama vowed to unite America. His signature lines drew knowing cheers at each new venue, leaving people nodding to one another, as though it was the first time they had ever heard them. "I'm not running for President of Red America or Blue America, or Black or White America. I'm running for President of the United States of America!" Obama events became sanctuaries where the races mixed easily and needed no special reason to strike up a conversation. Black kids sat next to whites, and the invisible barriers that often exist on trains, in colleges and in workplaces came tumbling down.

Third, Obama proposed to reduce the cost of going to college by giving financial credits in exchange for community volunteer work. This promise resonated loudly on university campuses.

But then, Barack Obama the community organiser got to work. Each time he finished speaking, Obama asked audience members to dial a number into their mobile phones. It was always 62262. Once people responded, he was in text-message communication with thousands of young new supporters – a tool Obama used to recruit volunteers and to remind students to vote on polling day.

"62262. Have you got it?" he asked the 19,000 packed into University of Maryland's Comcast Arena in February 2008. For

Obama, who began his career training people to recruit others, this may have been the single most important line of his stump speech. Words could inspire individuals, but tangible contact with volunteers and new voters could spread the message further. I signed up with all the candidates' campaigns, and received plenty of emails in return, but only Barack Obama sent regular text messages reminding me to watch his debates and log on to his website.

Without pausing for breath, Obama racked up a string of victories in February 2008, including the state of Washington where he won 68 per cent of the vote, Virginia 64 per cent, Maryland 61 per cent, and the District of Columbia 75 per cent. Continuing his winning streak, he took his home state of Hawaii, as well as Nebraska, Wisconsin, Maine and the Virgin Islands. Several of these were caucuses into which the Clinton campaign failed to put adequate resources. That was one of the Clinton campaign's sorriest miscalculations. "She should have made the same effort to win the caucus states that she made in primary states," said Max Brantley, editor of the *Arkansas Times*. "They didn't have sufficient grassroots organising among party faithful to turn out the people you needed to win caucuses."

Caucus states, where local people met and voted openly, rather than by secret ballot, typically yielded fewer delegates. Yet they would prove to be Obama's crucial advantage in the final months when the difference between Clinton and Obama remained stubbornly stuck at 150-200 delegates. Once Obama pulled ahead in "pledged delegates" – those actually won in primary contests – the "superdelegates" followed suit.

In the American electoral system, superdelegates are congressmen, senators, governors, former presidents and senior party officials who – based on their elevated status alone – are entitled to vote for a candidate at the Democratic convention. In 2008, there were close to 800 superdelegates, including big names like Bill Clinton, Jimmy Carter and Al Gore. Historically, the idea behind superdelegates was that they acted as a check-and-balance on the party in case there was disagreement over the candidate selected by the people. In 2008, however, they played a critical role because of the closeness of the race. Hillary Clinton started out with more superdelegates backing her, but as the marathon campaign wore on, a majority shifted to Obama.

By mid-February, the whiff of inevitability that had surrounded the Clinton campaign just six weeks earlier was gone. The once formidable and feared Clinton machine was busy retooling itself as the "scrappy underdog" doing battle with the might of the Obama behemoth. In November 2007, Republican David Keane of the American Conservative Union told me that Clinton's machine would be hard to beat, even in the general election. "It has the reputation of being one of the meanest networks on the block," Keane said. Twelve weeks later, the Clinton campaign was fighting for its life – one of the most stunning turnarounds in American political history. "Here's a black guy from Chicago who sits down in a room two years ago and says, 'I can beat the Clintons'. I think he would have got a hundred to one," said *Irish Voice* editor Niall O'Dowd looking back. "They were underestimating to a critical degree what it would take to win the primaries," he said, referring to Clinton's team.

But Hillary Clinton had been down too many times before to walk away in defeat. In 1992, she might have crawled under a stone when Gennifer Flowers, a lounge singer, almost derailed Bill Clinton's bid for the presidency by playing tapes of him whispering sweet nothings over the phone. But Hillary Clinton stood by her man, and the couple came through it. Again, when President Clinton declared, "I did not have sexual relations with that woman Miss Lewinsky," Hillary lashed out at the "vast rightwing conspiracy" she believed was probing every aspect of their lives. With her backing and her grace, they survived a second time. "She really did see her presidential ambitions going down the drain," said Sally Bedell Smith of the drama that engulfed the White House in 1998. "I think that certainly was a factor in keeping them together during what was a public humiliation for her throughout that whole episode." Now that Hillary Clinton was down again, it was time to go on the attack against Barack Obama.

Mark Penn drew up a new strategy to paint Obama as weak and untested in a crisis. Since Texas and Ohio were the next states to vote in early March, the Clinton campaign came up with a television advertisement depicting a 3 a.m. phone call to the White House. The question asked was who voters would want answering the call. Comedy shows loved it. In the first of a series of opinion altering parodies of the candidates, *Saturday Night Live* performed a sketch depicting a President Barack Obama answering the crisis phone call and promptly phoning Mrs Clinton to come and help him.

Americans joked that if "President" Hillary Clinton heard the White House phone ring at 3 a.m., her first thought would be, "What has Bill done now?" But skits aside, the message had worked.

A solid win in Ohio and a squeaker in Texas brought Hillary Clinton's campaign roaring back to life. With those big states under her belt, Clinton broke Obama's winning streak and cast doubt on the outcome of the race. Obama still had young and minority voters behind him, but with the white working class Mrs Clinton discovered a new constituency. Armed with fresh impetus, she was off and running to the new battlefield of Pennsylvania. Unfortunately, Clinton got her war zones all mixed up,

"I remember landing under sniper fire," Clinton told a Pennsylvania audience, recounting an official trip to Bosnia in 1996 as the First Lady. "There was supposed to be some kind of greeting ceremony at the airport, but instead we just ran with our heads down to get into the vehicles and get to our base." The story was meant to showcase the practical and hair-raising nature of Clinton's foreign policy experience, but her memory of arriving in Tuzla, Bosnia, was jumbled. That night, news channels produced footage from 1996 showing the then First Lady and daughter Chelsea calmly making their way from the plane to a small, friendly welcoming ceremony. There had been no ducking, no bullets and no snipers. "So I made a mistake," she told reporters. "It proves I'm human."

With a start like that, Clinton needed to dive for cover in Pennsylvania. So she headed for the northeastern town of Scranton, where her paternal grandfather was raised. Clinton's roots gave her an instant connection to the city's people, and jovial Pennsylvania governor Ed Rendell became a powerful cheerleader for her candidacy. Far from the sniping of the mainstream media, she had found a comfort zone. Pennsylvania, with its high number of Irish Catholics, liked Hillary Clinton.

By contrast, Barack Obama was still considered to be foreign exotica in the blue-collar state and harder to sell to people who wanted things to be the way they were in the 1990s before well-paid steel and manufacturing jobs disappeared. Then, an off-the-cuff comment put the African-American senator at the centre of his own media storm. "They get bitter and they cling to guns or religion, or antipathy to people who aren't like them," he said at a high dollar fundraising event in San Francisco. Obama was speaking about small-town Americans, hurt by job losses – the very voters he needed to attract.

For a candidate who had studiously avoided inserting his foot into his mouth, this was a rare misstep. Not only did it show Obama speaking to wealthy Californians about small town folks behind their backs, but it also introduced God and guns into an election that up that point had been free of either. Hillary Clinton took full advantage and called her opponent "elitist and out of touch".

As the argument played nationally, the small-town Pennsylvanians I met remained ambivalent. As long as Obama was not planning to take away their guns or their God, most could not care less about his views. "I think if everybody had a gun, there would be less crime around here," a man remarked to me in the town of York, where a sizable number of residents slide by on welfare. The young Pennsylvanian was on the side of those Americans who believe that "gun control" only takes guns away from law-abiding citizens and not from criminals. Margaret Eccles Ray, who moved from New York City to open a mobile phone store in York, sided with Obama. "What he was talking about was what we've all been talking about. We need to do something different. We need to put the joy back into being an American, and embrace the positive, not the negative," she said, telling me that in her opinion Obama simply had spoken the truth.

With days to go before the Pennsylvania vote, Hillary Clinton knocked back a shot of whiskey and popped off a gun Annie Oakley-style. Somehow, both candidates' personae had become muddled. Obama, raised by a single mother who sometimes depended on food stamps, became the elitist. Whereas Clinton, who together with her husband had earned $100 million since leaving the White House in 2001, became the reigning champion of the gun-toting middle class. Political campaigns had a funny way of coming up with the unexpected. One day you were dodging bullets, the next day you were calling the shots.

Caitríona Fitzpatrick's internship with Hillary Clinton's campaign ended after the victories in Texas and Ohio, and Caitríona went back to Ireland. "It was good to leave on a high," she told me from Dublin where she continued to work in Irish politics. For the final few weeks, Fitzpatrick had moved out of the Arlington, Virginia office to campaign door-to-door in Cleveland, Ohio, which is home to a large Irish-American population. "Anyone with a surname of Murphy I could be talking to," Caitríona laughed. "You'd go into pubs to recruit volunteers and talk about the difference the Clintons made to Ireland." The hours were long and, as polling day approached, nobody slept. "One day in Ohio we finished up at two in the morning, and the guy running it turned around and said, 'See you at five!'"

Caitríona Fitzpatrick feels that because they all worked so hard, the campaign staff did not notice that Hillary Clinton was chasing an inevitable loss. In the bubble, everything was positive and the idea of losing was not entertained. "I came home and started reading Denis Staunton in *The Irish Times*, and it was much different to what I had been reading over there. It took a while for my mind to come around and say, 'OK, I think I was on a completely different planet when I was there'."

Looking at the election from a distance, Caitríona wondered if Americans were seeking something they had lost nearly fifty years ago. "They want someone they can hold up," Fitzpatrick said, believing American voters in 2008 craved a president like John F. Kennedy. whose picture they could place on the mantelpiece. "Obama seemed to represent that more. He was so similar to Kennedy," she said.

On 22 April 2008 Hillary Clinton won the Pennsylvania primary, capping a run of victories in important electoral states. But despite Clinton's arguments that she was now the best placed to win an election against John McCain – who had become the Republican nominee in March – Democratic support continued to drift slowly towards Barack Obama. For Hillary Clinton, victory was a bit like the sniper fire in Bosnia. She was sure she could feel it and hear it. But it was not really there at all.

6

Kentucky Blues

*"It's not just Kentucky bluegrass that's music to my ears.
It's the sound of your overwhelming confidence in the face
of some really tough odds."* – HILLARY CLINTON

O N A SATURDAY MORNING IN MAY 2008, Senator Edward Kennedy returned from walking his dogs at the family compound in Hyannis Port and suffered a seizure. He was airlifted to hospital in Boston, and all that weekend newscasts buzzed with speculation about a possible stroke or heart attack. It was not Kennedy's first health scare. In 2007, he had undergone surgery to remove plaque that was narrowing his carotid artery but only days later appeared before cameras eating ice cream. The "Lion of the Senate" was not yet out of the political game.

This time he was not so lucky. After days of testing, it was announced that Kennedy was suffering from an aggressive form of brain cancer. For a man of seventy-six years, it was grim news. Within the halls of power in Washington and across America, there was a prevailing sense that another legendary Kennedy career was ending. Rather than hitting the campaign trail for Barack Obama, Ted Kennedy would undergo neurosurgery and spend precious time with his family.

Something else was winding down that week, but not in a way that was easy to understand. Hillary Clinton's bid to become the forty-fourth president of the United States was almost out of gas. Ironically, she lost the race despite winning the last few primary contests by huge margins. So while Barack Obama was almost certain to be the Democratic nominee, the people of West Virginia gave him a big "thumbs down" and now Kentucky was about to do the same.

Pollsters routinely described voters in states like West Virginia and Kentucky as "uneducated whites". It sounded pretty much like "stupid white people" – a discourteous description of any demographic – and one that warranted further scrutiny. I sensed the Kentucky primary might be my last opportunity to see Hillary Clinton on the campaign trail, so I flew to Louisville and checked into the downtown Holiday Inn.

Louisville is one of those flat cities with big wide streets and a fast food joint on every corner. You need only be there five minutes to know that Colonel Sanders, the man who pioneered Kentucky Fried Chicken, is a local hero. There is, however, something "old world" about the place. My hotel had borrowed its decor from the 1970s, nobody moves fast, and the people are friendly and polite. While Louisville is no architectural paradise, the warm breeze blowing through the streets in late May made it a comfortable city to explore. After two hours walking, it was time to find Hillary Clinton.

By now, I had perfected the knack of avoiding suffocating press enclosures at campaign events. I donned a "Hillary for President" badge, joined the line of supporters outside the Marriott Hotel and headed for yet another ballroom. The Secret Service was at the door, but they must have been already in wind-down mode. They did not even see my radio equipment, which should have landed me back in the press pen. Or if they did, it was not an issue that evening.

Inside, campaign workers from various electoral precincts staked out spots close to the stage, hoping for a chance to press palms with Clinton. As results came in, they studied the Kentucky map on large television screens erected around the room, anxious to discover how their areas had performed. They need not have worried. In most areas, Hillary Clinton outpolled Barack Obama by more than two to one. It was a cakewalk.

Alberta Waddell Rudder was ecstatic. She had spent the previous two days working the phones and lighting candles for Hillary. Alberta's twin strategies paid off handsomely. "I set out the Blessed Virgin Mary statue, and every election I burn those candles," she told me, fixing her grey hair into a ponytail. This time she added prayers for Clinton. "Blessed Virgin Mary, you're a woman. Please help Hillary." Alberta had voted in each election since Dwight D. Eisenhower became president in 1952. But if Hillary Clinton did not become the Democratic nominee, this might be first time in fifty-six years that Alberta would stay away from the November polls. Barack Obama, she said, scared her. "There's nothing against him being a black man. In my heart, I'm frightened of him. Where's he come from? Where's he getting all this money all the time?"

Waddell Rudder had heard the same concerns from Kentuckians "back in the woods" whom she had canvassed on behalf of Hillary Clinton. "That's why I think Obama's going to lose. They are afraid of him, and I think the Reverend Wright had a lot to do with putting that fear in people," Alberta said, referring to Obama's pastor in Chicago. Stoking fears that his church was a radical anti-white outfit, the Reverend Jeremiah Wright had shouted "God damn America" during a 2003 sermon captured on video and replayed hundreds of times on television. Wright was referring to what he saw as America's mistreatment of its black population. At first, Barack Obama stood by the pastor who had married him and baptised his children. "I can no more disown him than my white grandmother," Obama said. But Wright had continued to talk out of turn, and eventually Obama resigned from Trinity United Church. Barack Obama did not join another church during the presidential campaign.

The term "blue-collar" means taking a manual job after school and holding it for as many years as possible. The man I met next was a pure, blue-collar Kentuckian. For seventeen years Jim worked at the local Ford car plant. Then for twenty-five more, he drove a truck for KFC Corporation – Kentucky Fried Chicken to the rest of us. Jim was just shy of five feet, with a mop of white hair and sad, tired eyes. "Everything was pretty stable when Bill was in there," he said, confirming that the memory of happier economic days under President Clinton helped deliver the Kentucky vote to Hillary. Now the Ford plant was letting people go and a steady pay packet was harder to come by. Bill Clinton was no liability around here. If anything, the former president was his wife's finest asset. "I think he did a good job," Jim contended.

"Was Obama considered to be too elitist in Kentucky?" I asked Jim's son Mikey, who was drinking beer with his dad. "Too what?" asked Mikey. "You know, the wine-sipping, high-minded type?" I asked again. "No, not that. He is just inexperienced. Period. I mean, what's he done? He was a real estate attorney up there in Chicago. Ran into some money. Had a guy that backed him. Ran a Senate thing for a term and didn't even complete that." Mikey provided me with the potted version of Obama's biography as seen from much of Appalachia. It had large gaps and a few inaccuracies. But for someone who had not been to Harvard and whose main worry was how to feed his family on less money, it was all Mikey wanted to know. He didn't want a President Barack Obama.

"Would you vote for Obama if he's the nominee?" I inquired of an older man, who was enjoying a cigar and a drink in the hotel lobby. "No, I would not!" he said, spitting alcohol in all directions. "Why?" "You really don't want to know." He shook his head and pointed to my recorder. I switched it off, and the old fellow leaned towards me. "Lot of folks round here wouldn't vote for a black person," he whispered. He leaned back and resumed his drinking. In months of interviews he was the first to admit, at least to me, what many were thinking. Polls carried out that day in Kentucky showed that, for one in five voters, the colour of Barack Obama's skin *was* an issue.

As we waited for Hillary Clinton to arrive in the ballroom, Democratic strategist Donna Brazile appeared on the big TV screens, but the volume had been turned down. "Pity we can't hear her," I remarked to a man standing beside me. "The only thing I want to hear from that bitch is that all the votes will be counted," he shot back. A black American, Brazile sat on the Democratic National Committee which would meet the following weekend to resolve the thorny issue of Florida and Michigan.

Back in January, Florida and Michigan forfeited their delegates when they broke party rules by staging their primaries too early. Clinton beat Obama in both states, and now she was arguing that if the delegates were reinstated, she could clinch the nomination. "It's not fair," a young Hillary supporter agreed, claiming that Donna Brazile and the 800 party officials who would have votes at the Democratic convention were effectively controlling the nomination. "The superdelegates need to butt out, and let the people have their say!" he snarled.

In trying to keep her dream alive a little while longer, Clinton had come to the right place. These Kentuckians were her diehard supporters. Close to the stage, a middle-aged woman fainted but refused to leave the ballroom for fresh air so as not to miss Hillary's speech.

Hillary Clinton wore the same dark brown suit and turquoise necklace she had on the first night I watched her in Iowa six months earlier. Back then she had come alone, cautiously optimistic, but wary of standing beside her husband in case the voters saw Bill as too close to the presidency again. Tonight, as Mrs Clinton's hopes of attaining the crown faded against the glow of her Kentucky victory, both Bill and Chelsea joined her on stage. Bill Clinton, sporting a faraway look that seemed to suggest surrender, kissed his wife lightly on the cheek and then moved off to the side as Hillary took the microphone.

In a way, this campaign was a reversal of their previous roles. Bill had always been the one out front, lapping up the public adulation, while Hillary had been the trusted adviser behind the scenes. Over the past eighteen months, however, each had attempted to play the other's part but neither had really succeeded. Being seen and not heard was not Bill Clinton's strong suit. Through hundreds of appearances, Hillary had grown comfortable with crowds, but even in this crowd most eyes followed Bill and Chelsea.

"It's not just Kentucky bluegrass that's music to my ears. It's the sound of your overwhelming confidence in the face of some really tough odds," Hillary Clinton said, acknowledging that Barack Obama was still ahead in delegates. "I commend Senator Obama and his supporters. And while we continue to go toe to toe for this nomination, we do see eye to eye when it comes to the unity of our party to elect a Democratic president." With a note of resignation, Clinton explained why it had come to this. "We have been massively outspent," she said. By now the "Hillary '08" campaign was underwater to the tune of $15-20 million, and her personal investment in the race was $11 million. She was not the only one who had lost her shirt. At a campaign stop, Clinton met Dalton Hatfield, a Kentucky boy who had sold his bike and video games to raise $422 to get Hillary to the White House.

Hillary Clinton's unbeatable spirit had saved her many times. But the longer she hung on, the more the Democratic Party suffered. As the likely nominee, Barack Obama needed to convince Americans like Alberta Waddell Rudder to put out religious statues and light candles for him too. Obama would have to inspire confidence in blue-collar workers like Jim and his son Mikey, and he needed time to work on Heather French, a young "Miss Kentucky" who told me that if the Democrats did not choose Hillary Clinton, then she was "definitely a McCain voter". By late May, Hillary Clinton felt the pressure building to end her battle for the White House.

Making the switch from front-runner to being ushered out of the race is something no candidate prepares for. Though the writing was on the wall, somewhere in her most secretive thoughts Hillary Clinton still hoped that Obama's narrow lead might all be a mistake. "I don't think I ever really gave up until she gave up," said Stella O'Leary of the Irish American Democrats, who understood how much Clinton must have agonised during those final days of the primaries. As she concluded her speech in Louisville that night, Hillary Clinton flipped the narrative one last time, just in case there was still a big banana skin waiting to send Obama sliding out of the race. "This continues to be a tough fight, and I have fought it the only way I know how – with determination, by never giving up and never giving in," she told us. "That's why I'm still running."

As a country music tune played out across the speaker system, Clinton waved off Kentucky with a mixed message. Her star was dimming, but she would fight to the end. Bill Clinton, a realist who knew that his wife's goose was cooked, stirred from his red-faced paralysis to shake hands and sign autographs. And twenty-eight-year-old Chelsea, a New York hedge fund employee, thanked local campaign workers. Too exhausted to greet more than a row or two of well-wishers, Hillary Clinton left her family to mop up the remaining handshakes and photographs.

THE FOLLOWING MORNING I WALKED through Louisville to the Ohio River, a vast grey-green torrent of water. On the north bank is Indiana, but from where I stood in the Red state of Kentucky, I could tell the time on a big clock over in the electoral battleground state of Indiana. A wayward tree stump hurtled down the Ohio River, and I descended to the windy bank to see about getting a ride on one of the steamboats preserved for tourists. As a traveller, there are odd days when I feel I have reached the heart of America. That day in Louisville I toured the numerous "wig and hat" shops in the black section of town. I saw that O'Rourke from Ireland is a big business name in the same town where Muhammad Ali grew up. I watched Salvadoran immigrants eating their lunch in a scrapyard, and exchanged greetings with a bare-chested man jogging across the bridge from Kentucky to Indiana. There were too many narratives here to fit one precise definition. The term "uneducated whites" could never fully describe Louisville, never mind Kentucky.

At the riverside, I learned I was not the first to wander down to the Ohio in search of answers. A sign on the dock told me that I had stumbled in behind a long list of curious minds. Among them were Charles Dickens in 1842, Abraham Lincoln in 1841, and Alexis de Tocqueville who had come here in 1831. That last name got me wondering what the Frenchman might have written if he were in Louisville today.

Most of the inhabitants I found to be hard-working people who supported the first female candidate for president because they had achieved the gift of prosperity under her husband William Clinton a decade earlier. Mr Obama was principally a stranger, who did not inspire their trust, and a small portion of the citizenry admitted to racist feelings. However, I had the sense that America was about to be swept upriver by a tide of change.

THE CLOSING STAGE OF THE BATTLE between Hillary Clinton and Barack Obama was fought in slow motion over the next few days. No one made any sudden movements. If anything, Clinton's exit became a dance in which she chose the final steps.

"We all remember that Bobby Kennedy was assassinated in June in California," she told the *Sioux Falls Argus Leader* in South Dakota, defending her decision to fight to the finish. In a moment of frankness – or exhaustion – Clinton let her most private thoughts escape. The Bobby Kennedy analogy struck a raw nerve with African-Americans, many of whom still feared that Obama could "be taken out". The Kennedy family and the Obamas decided not to make an issue out of it. After all, Hillary Clinton was conceding that in order to win the nomination she needed something of that magnitude – an assassination – to occur. For his part, Barack Obama had already moved ahead and was sparring with John McCain.

On the weekend of 1 June 2008, the Democratic National Committee, led by the former presidential candidate Howard Dean, met to discuss a solution to problem of the Florida and Michigan delegates. On Clinton's behalf, Harold Ickes argued that denying the two states their delegates at the Democratic convention was "undemocratic". The party held firm. Even former Clinton loyalists spoke out against the proposal to reinstate the delegates – a final sign, if one were needed, that the Democratic Party was eyeing a future without the Clintons in charge. As a compromise, it was decided to seat half of Florida and Michigan's delegates at the Denver convention. The nomination had been moved further towards Barack Obama.

Obama won the final state of Montana on 3 June, pushing him over the 2,118 delegates needed to clinch the nomination. "Tonight I can stand and say that I will be the Democratic nominee for president of the United States," Obama declared. After five months of combat across fifty-six separate primary elections, the forty-six-year-old had emerged the winner and made history as the first African-American nominee for president. Barack Obama won 1,766 pledged delegates, only 127 more than Clinton's 1,639, and he made up the balance with support from superdelegates. Though some states never reported popular vote totals, one independent estimate put Obama's likely vote total at 17.6 million, just 50,000 above Clinton's.

The epic nature of Barack Obama's victory was lost in the continuing drama that played out in New York. Rather than concede immediately, Clinton congratulated her opponent but did not suspend her campaign. "I want the nearly eighteen million people who voted for me to be respected," she said, leading to speculation that Clinton's support for Obama would be contingent on receiving concessions, perhaps including the number two spot on the ticket. Talk in political circles was that Bill Clinton now saw the vice-presidency as Hillary's most likely route to the presidency.

The day after Obama's Montana primary victory, Clinton came under renewed pressure from within the Democratic Party to get behind Obama. In conference calls with key supporters in Congress and her home state of New York, Hillary Clinton was urged to concede as soon as possible. Massachusetts Representative Barney Frank and New York's own Representative Charles Rangel both encouraged Clinton to end her quest for the presidency. "I'm moving in that direction," was how *Newsweek* reported Clinton's response.

A day later my email in-tray contained a message from Hillary Clinton. I had signed on to her website and periodically received "personalised" emails from the candidate. This one read: "Dear Carole, I wanted you to be one of the first to know. On Saturday, I will extend my congratulations to Senator Obama and declare my support for his candidacy." I was on holidays when I received the email, and I watched Clinton bow out of the presidential race from a pub on Achill Island. For a minute, the place went silent as patrons absorbed the news. Then someone switched the television back to a football match that was generating huge excitement.

THE SOUL-SEARCHING ABOUT HOW a newcomer bested the First Lady of American politics didn't last long, and Americans soon re-focused on Obama. In the end, voters chose "change" over "experience". The Bush White House had plenty of experience but had delivered many spectacular failures. The Clinton team's initial thought that "We are more Thatcher than anyone else" did not fit America's needs in 2008. The country was not looking for a Thatcher. It wanted the hope of a JFK. With the correct message, Barack Obama had simply outwitted his opponents by using the internet to efficiently organise young people and bring in almost $280 million in campaign cash to fight the primaries.

Unflattering media coverage may have hindered Hillary Clinton in 2008, particularly what Karl Frish of the online *Media Matters* website described as "sexist rants" against her. "When Hillary Clinton comes on television, I involuntarily cross my legs," famously said former MSNBC host Tucker Carlson. "People seemed to be more candid than we expected them to be about their dislike of her," agreed Letifa Lyles of the National Organisation for Women, who saw sexism working against Clinton from the start of the campaign. "It's clear it makes people very uncomfortable still – the notion of a woman as president, as Commander-in-Chief," Lyles said.

Others believed that Bill Clinton should have stayed out of the race instead of dashing in to try to save his wife at the first sign of vulnerability. "It was only when Obama emerged as a serious contender that they unleashed him, and that's when all the trouble happened," said Sally Bedell Smith. In the public's mind, the former president took some of the blame for the loss of support among African-Americans. Months later Bill Clinton acknowledged that there were some things "I wish I hadn't said". But he forcefully denied that in describing Obama as "inexperienced", or comparing him to former presidential candidate Jessie Jackson during the South Carolina primary, he had intended any insult. "I am not a racist," Bill Clinton said. "I didn't attack him personally."

Ultimately, it may have been Hillary Clinton's 2002 Senate vote for the Iraq war that sank her. In a country that had turned against the war, Clinton could not escape her initial vote supporting the invasion. Her story that "if we had known then what we know now" didn't cut any ice, since she had neglected to read the National Intelligence Estimate provided to members of Congress before the vote. That document, prepared by US intelligence, had cast serious doubt on the existence of weapons of mass destruction in Iraq.

"The presumption of victory was ill-founded," concluded Irish-American fundraiser Declan Kelly, who believed that Clinton's White House bid failed not because the candidate herself was arrogant, but because the campaign made tactical errors, such as neglecting small states, which ultimately made the difference. "Obama won because he ran a better campaign. He deserved to win," said Kelly.

To clear the debt amassed during the bruising primary battle, Clinton continued fundraising. At their first joint appearance after the primaries, Barack Obama tentatively agreed to assist Hillary Clinton with her debt. To win favour, he even wrote a personal cheque for the maximum allowable contribution of $2,300 in front of her financial backers. "He seemed like he was concerned that he might be attacked," said Stella O'Leary, who was present at that late June 2008 meeting at the Mayflower Hotel in Washington DC. "It was very tense," O'Leary said, recalling this first attempt at Democratic unity.

It was unclear if Hillary Clinton wanted to be Barack Obama's vice-president as badly as her supporters did. But, from the start, Barack Obama seemed cool to the idea. If Obama chose Clinton, he and key advisers felt ex-president Bill Clinton would be always sitting on his shoulder. As the summer progressed, the possibility of an Obama-Clinton dream ticket began to fade.

Short of being offered a key cabinet position in an Obama administration, such as Secretary of State, observers agreed that Clinton would continue to build her career in the Senate. "Oh sure, what else does she have to do?" said *Arkansas Times* editor Max Brantley, an old acquaintance of the Clintons. "I don't think this campaign will harm her in New York one bit. She ought to be bulletproof in terms of re-election to the Senate." Regardless of whatever she chooses, Hillary Clinton will remain highly influential on Capitol Hill.

After his failed presidential bid in 1980, Massachusetts Senator Ted Kennedy, for example, returned to build an outstanding Senate career, resulting in what many believe is a greater legacy than some presidents. But Kennedy had toiled in the Senate for almost twenty years before seeking the Democratic nomination, and he considers Capitol Hill to be his true home.

"I loved the Senate before I ran for president," Ted Kennedy told the *Washington Post* in 2008. Losing to Jimmy Carter, he claimed, made him appreciate it all the more. "It all depends on the attitude, what's in the mind of the person," Kennedy concluded.

Though Hillary Clinton has commented that you should "bloom where you are planted", it is also still possible for her to make another run for the White House. After the primaries, she asked donors if they would agree to transfer contributions intended for her 2008 general election to a new 2012 fund. That money could be used for a third New York Senate campaign in 2012, or it could become seed money for another presidential run in 2012, or even in 2016 when Mrs Clinton would be sixty-eight.

"She'll be younger than McCain is today in eight years. She's a vigorous and healthy person. She's got a long career ahead of her," said Brantley.

7

Backroom Business

"People left his talk looking at each other, and smiling at each other and signing up to do things." – OBAMA CAMPAIGNER

"Working for Hillary and helping her is something I would do a thousand times over." – CLINTON STAFFER

B Y EARLY JULY 2008 BURNS STRIDER was tapping away quietly on a computer in his office suite across the Potomac River from Washington DC. He did not expect to be starting a new venture so soon. If things had gone differently, the large man in his mid-forties – with a slow Mississippi drawl and shy smile – would still be at the old desk where for sixteen months he served as a senior adviser for Hillary Clinton's presidential race. Most days Strider had reported to work at campaign headquarters in nearby Arlington, Virginia, and loved his job selling Clinton to America's religious voters.

"I was an adviser to Nancy Pelosi in the House," the former Baptist missionary said, explaining how Speaker Pelosi and other Democrats had cottoned on to the need to show their "faithful side" instead of always letting Republicans run off with the religious vote. "Out of that, I had an opportunity to meet with Senator Clinton and join the campaign." Strider's face brightened at the thought of Hillary Clinton, as though he was missing her. "I like seeing her faith in action," he continued. "The Book of James says faith without works is dead, and I think that she embodies that."

Two doors up the corridor from Strider, I found his new business partner Patrick Lewis, another graduate of the Clinton campaign. Lewis, a fit-looking father of five with family connections in Waterford, was in the habit of giving a few hundred dollars to Democratic presidential candidates. But after the Al Gore and John Kerry losses to George W. Bush in 2000 and 2004, Lewis felt the urge to do more than write cheques. "You give money and then what?" he wondered aloud, explaining that this time – after evaluating the candidates and settling on Hillary Clinton – he had wound down his ten-year-old law practice and started volunteer work for her presidential bid.

Over at Clinton's Virginia election headquarters, Lewis ran into Strider, a paid staffer, and the two hit it off. Burns Strider was also liaising with generals and military top-brass, trying to get veterans interested in supporting Clinton. When Patrick Lewis mentioned that he had served in the Army, they made him Deputy Director for Veterans Outreach. Unlike most campaign staffers with such a grand title, Lewis chose to remain unpaid and put his law business "on ice" for a while. "By the time the primaries were in full swing, I had handed all the matters I was working on to other lawyers, or they had closed out naturally," Lewis said. He planned to work for Hillary Clinton through the early months of 2008, right up until her nomination. Then he would return to the campaign, later in the autumn, to help give her the final push towards the White House.

RORY FINNIN WAS ALSO LOOKING for a way to get involved in the Democratic presidential campaign when he met Barack Obama at a small gathering in Brooklyn in the summer of 2007. As a former Peace Corps worker in the Ukraine, Finnin had observed grassroots politics first-hand and was interested in seeing a president elected in America who would reignite such popular mobilisation. "Obama impressed me with the way he spoke about that," said Finnin. Sitting at the Brooklyn meeting, he thought that if Barack Obama could only get more people to hear his message about the importance of communities working together to get things done, Obama could win. Americans were hungry for a new way to get involved in government. "People left his talk looking at each other, and smiling at each other and signing up to do things."

The Finnin family is steeped in Irish culture. Rory's father emigrated to New York from Limerick, and as a boy Rory played both hurling and baseball. His growing intellectual interests, however, drew him to the former Soviet Union. In his twenties Finnin learned the Ukrainian language, and by 2007 he was immersed in a doctorate at New York's Columbia University. His chosen topic was the authors who chronicled Stalin's deportation of the Muslim Crimean Tatars. It was a far cry from knocking on doors in Iowa and New Hampshire, but after reading both Barack Obama's memoir and his second book *The Audacity of Hope*, in which Obama outlines his vision for a changed America, the thirty-five-year-old Finnin hit the campaign trail.

In the winter of 2007, being an Obama volunteer was a calling. For Finnin and those who joined him, it meant getting out of bed in New York City before dawn, piling into a rented car and driving across several states. The next step was checking into a cheap hotel and dropping in to a crowded local campaign office to find out which areas needed to be canvassed. "What really impressed me was the willingness of the staff to let us do our own thing," said Finnin. Travelling across the country, Obama volunteers paid their own expenses, drove their own cars, and regularly slept nights on floors just to the have opportunity to go door to door as advocates for Obama. "There wasn't tight control over our activity. I was told to take initiative, and I did so. We all felt like leaders." As long as they stuck to the candidate's philosophy – which was to "respect, empower and include" everyone they met – canvassers like Rory Finnin could make their own pitch on each voter's doorstep. The chief caveat was that they should not speak negatively about Obama's rivals.

From the time of the Iowa caucus in January 2008, thousands of students from all fifty states similarly signed up to spend their weekends canvassing. As Obama's ability to inspire young people grew, their numbers doubled and then trebled. Students took time away from college, graduates abandoned job searches, and some full-time employees left their jobs to devote time to the election. The Obama campaign came along at a defining moment in American history, but the huge numbers of young people willing to sacrifice and economise for months on end brought Obama's team much added energy and enthusiasm.

There were other ways to get a first-hand look at democracy in action. By contributing $4,600 to the Clinton campaign, donors earned the distinction of becoming a "Hill Star". These generous souls were rewarded with weekend volunteer opportunities manning phone banks or canvassing neighbourhoods. Some "Hill Stars" took the opportunity seriously and worked around the clock. Others saw the weekends as social outings or a chance for a photograph with the candidate.

Back at Clinton headquarters, Burns Strider was among nearly 1,000 full-time employees who formed the core of the election team. Hillary Clinton started out with a considerably larger staff than Barack Obama, roughly 600 to his 200 paid employees, but as the Illinois senator garnered large amounts of cash, he took in more people too. For his national headquarters, Obama selected a Michigan Avenue high-rise in downtown Chicago and used the skills he had learned as a community organiser to build a new grassroots election movement. Chicago volunteer Mike Kruglik, who worked with Obama in the 1980s, described the 2008 strategy as "an unprecedented combination of central control and guidance, along with opportunity for people to create their own campaign within the larger campaign". Working on Barack Obama's staff gave these individuals essential skills to manage their own campaigns, and after the primaries many Obama volunteers ran for local office themselves.

Barack Obama's knack for organising "from the ground up" was evident well before his first primary triumph in Iowa. Before Obama danced in the full glare of the media spotlight, his team spent long months training volunteers in the inner workings of little understood caucus meetings. "There's a tendency among journalists to follow the candidate, not the campaign," said Rory Finnin, explaining how Obama's victory was put together by learning the process of the caucus meeting, then simply teaching others how to pass it on. "People were leaders, constantly building a network that became so numerous and so energised that seeing them in the caucus rooms being able to communicate Obama's message was very powerful."

As CLINTON'S TOP ADVISER ON THE religious vote, part of Burns Strider's job was to set up appearances for the candidate at churches across America. A big coup was getting Bill and Hillary Clinton a joint appearance at Saddleback, an Evangelical mega-church in southern California. Meeting with Pastor Rick Warren of Saddleback gave Hillary Clinton an opportunity to address the religious right who were not in love with the Republican choices, including John McCain, despite his impeccable pro-life record. Hillary Clinton also visited countless churches across the South, where she courted African-Americans and where journalists teased her for using a southern accent to match her husband's. Bill Clinton, with his preacher-like qualities, had always resonated well with religious voters.

On the road for weeks at a time, Patrick Lewis rounded up supportive military veterans to personally meet Hillary Clinton at local rallies. "My job was to find veterans and get them there," Lewis said. "We had a big fifteen-passenger van with 'Vets for Hillary' painted on the side just driving around trying to drum up interest." Sometimes Lewis just dropped into the Veterans of Foreign Wars club on the edge of a new town and shared a drink with the locals. "We'd go as members or guests, displaying our 'Hillary for President' buttons. It wasn't hard to start a conversation about politics!"

If the tray of half-eaten hamburgers left outside Hillary Clinton's hotel door back in Des Moines, Iowa, was any indication of life on the road for a presidential candidate, it was not five-star travel. Marianne Pernold, who questioned Clinton at a town hall meeting in Portsmouth, New Hampshire, said Hillary Clinton told her that most nights she ate pizza for dinner. As for a gym, she had not seen the inside of one for months.

"I hadn't had that type of lifestyle since I was in the Army," Patrick Lewis confirmed. As the race tightened, taking a weekend off was out of the question for campaign workers, and family birthdays and anniversaries went by the wayside. "Not knowing where you are going to sleep the next night, it's just a daze," Lewis said, trying to recall for me where he had travelled and in what month.

To exist inside a presidential campaign is to live in what political consultants and strategists sometimes call a "war room". Though insiders say this war is not so much about defeating enemies as about achieving positive goals, all campaigns play the detective on one another. Opposition researchers are employed to dig up opponents' voting records and hunt for any misdeeds that escape the media's attention. Such researchers are part and parcel of modern electoral warfare, and in 2008 all the candidates had them. These days, ordinary supporters conduct research and phone tips into campaign hotlines in the hope that they also can help hobble an opponent. And when reporters are not present to catch a candidate's gaffes, Joe Public is forever on duty with his camera phone and ready to upload video clips to YouTube. One of Barack Obama's rare misstatements – about how small-town Americans "cling to guns and religion" – was recorded and brought to national media attention by an ordinary citizen at one of Obama's own fundraisers.

For Rory Finnin, who volunteered for Barack Obama in several states during the spring of 2008, the camaraderie between ground crews was usually friendly. But as the race between Obama and Clinton tightened, it was inevitable that volunteers from both camps would meet out on the streets. Sometimes tempers flared. "In New York, I remember very vividly marching from Harlem down to Columbus Circle. We were chanting 'Obama '08! Be Part of Something Great!'" There was a counter-protest of Clinton volunteers, who as they walked by, kind of taunted us. I couldn't imagine Obama volunteers doing that," Finnin recalled.

But I had witnessed primary night crowds where news of a Clinton victory had been greeted with loud "boos" from Obama supporters, and I had been at Clinton rallies where exasperated campaigners would just as soon not mention Barack Obama at all. At the height of the primary season, competitive hostility was almost certainly a shared emotion.

BY MARCH, WHEN CLINTON FELT a white working-class wind behind her, both Strider and Lewis were put to the pin-of-their-collars to turn out religious voters in big numbers. "We had remarkable success in Catholic neighbourhoods, largely due to the Clintons," said Burns Strider. "It was just a matter of sharing their story, letting voters know where and when to vote, and making sure that they did." Strider, however, comes from the Baptist tradition, the Clintons are Methodist, and Lewis is the only Catholic. But with plenty of help on the ground, the two managed to form a solid connection with Catholic voters in Ohio and Pennsylvania – some of the same voters Barack Obama would need to secure the presidency in November.

At Clinton headquarters, Burns Strider sat at the senior table. He was in on the meetings with Hillary Clinton's top five advisers and witnessed the ups and downs as Obama pulled ahead. "Was Hillary Clinton running the campaign, or was it running her?" I asked Strider, hoping for some insight into reported temper explosions inside the Clinton war room. "It was a presidential campaign structure. She was the candidate, and she was in charge," he insisted bluntly.

Patrick Lewis, speaking from a volunteer perspective, was freer with his interpretation of how Clinton's campaign had failed to meet the Obama challenge. "I think a programme was put in place that she helped put together, and it took a while to re-evaluate it," Lewis said. "She was still running a programme even after she realised it wasn't connecting the way she had anticipated." Hillary Clinton learned late in the process that she would have to fight on beyond 5 February, the date by which she had originally hoped to become the Democratic nominee. Having run early as the candidate of "experience", Clinton found her new niche as a middle-class heroine too late in the day. Barack Obama had already captivated voters with the simple idea of "change".

Even in the dying days of the primaries, Hillary Clinton and her team gave pep talks to keep staff and volunteers fully invested and believing that victory was possible. "Not in a cynical fashion," Patrick Lewis recalled. "Not 'you better say that you think she can still win because you work here'. We all really felt she had a chance." Again, despite the mountain of media coverage that Clinton had received over the last two decades, which turned her into one of world's best-known faces, political insiders still lamented how far removed her public image was from the caring woman they had each come to know. "I think every story should be positive," said Burns Strider, who had worked with Hillary Clinton on eradicating malaria and AIDS in Africa.

"No nonsense" was how Pat Lewis described the candidate he spent months volunteering for, something he suspected outsiders often confused with Nixonian nastiness. "She just doesn't want to talk about anything that isn't focused on achieving what's before her," he said. Both Patrick Lewis and

Burns Strider believed that the American media ultimately became entranced by the amazing story of Barack Obama.

THE CLINTON CAMPAIGN ENDED DIFFERENTLY for the two insiders. As the delegate mathematics began to look increasingly problematic, Patrick Lewis backed away. "I saw the math too. I started re-engaging my law practice at that point. I had the luxury of being able to do it. Others who worked for her, they still had a job they had to do. By the time April rolled around, I needed to reconnect with my life."

By then Hillary Clinton was barrelling into Pennsylvania hoping a big victory there could put her ahead of Barack Obama. "At what stage did you know it wasn't going to happen for her?" I asked Strider. "We were in it up until the very end," he said, giving nothing away. "It could not have been easy," I persisted, "knowing at some point that Obama would emerge the winner." He still did not bite. "If I was feeling tired or overworked, all I had to do was look at Senator Clinton and realise that she was working harder and going longer. That did it for me. I kept going," Strider replied.

Since the Clinton election machine was still winding down when I ran into Strider, I wondered if he was still "on-message" and just reluctant to reveal anything that would hurt the campaign. But before I left his office, I had changed my mind. "Are you relieved to be getting back to normal life?" I asked. "No," he replied without hesitation. "I'm enjoying getting to know my children again and taking my wife out on a few dates, but working for Hillary and helping her is something I would do a thousand times over." Advising Hillary Clinton had not just been an income for Burns Strider. He had been a true believer in Clinton's ability to lead America into the future.

Strider and Lewis, I believe, would have been able to work equally as hard for Barack Obama if they had been asked to join his growing campaign staff. With his religious contacts, Burns Strider would be invaluable to any political candidate, and Patrick Lewis could get "Vets for Obama" painted on the side of the minivan. But like many others fresh off the Clinton campaign trail, the men found that that most of the slots in "Obamaland" were taken. Instead, they joined forces and set up a new venture advising political candidates across America how to win over religious voters. By the autumn of 2008, business was booming.

BACK IN NEW YORK, RORY FINNIN was packing for another trip. After a winter and spring spent sleeping in motels and knocking on doors for Barack Obama, Finnin's Slavic side was calling him again. He was offered a job as a lecturer in Ukrainian studies at Cambridge University, and felt he could not pass up the opportunity. "It's hard to leave now because we are needed even more," Finnin said, referring to what he expected would be a major Republican onslaught against Obama as the presidential election approached. "The Republican side is quite frightened of the way this candidate has mobilised people."

Since Barack Obama first announced his candidacy in early 2007, teams of volunteers had registered millions of new voters. Up to 2008, almost 50 per cent of Americans did not normally vote. So, in one of the biggest efforts since the 1960s to move people on to the voting rolls, recruiters stood outside sports arenas and rock concerts signing up every new voter they could find. While both the Democratic and Republican candidates benefited from having more Americans on the register, a clear majority of first-time voters signed up as Democrats. "That energy is a target for the other side," Finnin said, expecting the Republicans to respond with an unprecedented registration drive of their own.

Like Barack Obama, Rory Finnin is tall and plays basketball, so "hoops" is what they talked about when they met briefly in Iowa. "I made a crack about joining him in a pick-up game," says Finnin, who claims he identified with Obama and his wife Michelle in a way he could not have done with any of the other candidates. "My wife and I are paying off our school loans, and we knew they had just finished paying off theirs. We relate to them," he said of the Obamas. "They have been thrust into the spotlight, but I kind of see them among our friends. I see them as normal people who want to do some good."

Having spent a year volunteering on behalf of Barack Obama, Rory Finnin left for England in July 2008 with a sense that he had played a small part in changing America. "I saw the way this grassroots thing was operating, and it worked. That was really very moving." Rory would miss the politics, but he had located a group of Obama supporters at Cambridge with whom he could share the highs and lows of the final months. He planned to return to the United States to help out closer to polling day. Though reluctant to jinx the campaign by speaking too soon, he had tentatively marked 20 January 2009 on his calendar. "I'd like to be back in town if he's inaugurated," Finnin said.

8

What Are Candidates Made Of?

"As the massive steel doors loudly clanked shut behind me, I felt a deeper dread than I have ever felt since." – JOHN MCCAIN, ON BECOMING A POW

"I'm LeBron, baby. I've got some game. I can play at this level." – BARACK OBAMA, BEFORE ADDRESSING THE 2004 DEMOCRATIC CONVENTION

MY HOME IN Annapolis, Maryland, looks directly across at the United States Naval Academy. The elite military college, which is home to 4,000 naval officers-in-training, fronts onto the Chesapeake Bay and is separated from the rest of city by a high wall. The midshipmen, dressed in their gleaming white naval uniforms in summer and black in winter, are a common sight in and around Annapolis. I have never seen a midshipman scale the Academy wall, but back in the mid-1950s students seeking illicit recreation in the city would sometimes sneak out by climbing across the high perimeter to freedom. The first one over the wall was usually John McCain.

"It was a high risk venture," recalled Frank Gamboa, a fellow midshipman who roomed with the future presidential candidate for three of their four years at the Naval Academy. Fifty years later he could spend a week churning up old stories about the man known to his Academy classmates back then as "John Wayne McCain".

"His manly style and his lady-killer reputation," Gamboa claimed, were responsible for the nickname. "He dated very attractive women who had lots of friends – so we hung around him, hoping we would be able to date some of their friends," said the former roommate.

John McCain came to Annapolis in 1954 with the knowledge that his life as a US Naval Officer had been preordained. Not only had his father attended the Naval Academy, but his grandfather too was a 1906 graduate. A profane old sea dog known as Admiral "Slew" McCain, John's grandfather had commanded US forces in the Pacific. John's father, Captain "Jack" McCain, had been the Navy liaison to Congress and in 1967 during the Vietnam War became an admiral and commander of American forces. As for John Sydney McCain III, there was no escaping the fact that much was expected of the young midshipman. "I think he resented not having a real option," Frank Gamboa opined. "He wanted to have a life on his terms, rather than have it dictated by family legacy. So it was a struggle for him."

In his autobiography, *Faith of My Fathers*, John McCain wrote that for his few first weeks in Annapolis he did well – before rebelling against the rigid system of discipline imposed on midshipmen by upperclassmen or senior students. "Our physical appearance was expected to conform to a code with rules so numerous, esoteric and pointless that I thought them absurd. We were commanded to perform dozens of menial tasks a day, each one intended to be more demeaning than the last, and made all the more so by the heap of verbal abuse that would accompany it."

John McCain lagged behind academically, devoting more time and attention to his social life than his studies. He loved history but struggled with mathematics and accumulated demerits for everything from his sloppy appearance to his daring escapades across the Academy wall. Frank Gamboa remembered McCain's father visiting the room they shared with two other midshipmen and knocking some sense into his son. "He happened to drop by our room when we were having a water fight, so we were all soaking wet in our under-shorts. The water fight had been started by John," recalled Gamboa with a laugh. "He told us our room was in gross disorder. He had John come down and meet with him in the rotunda for a little counselling!"

Throughout his political career, John McCain acquired the moniker of "Maverick". In 2006, McCain openly questioned George Bush's handling of the Iraq war and pushed for extra troops to quell the growing violence there. He opposed his party on climate change, campaign finance and the torture of prisoners captured by American forces abroad. But John McCain also took risks that were sometimes breathless in their audacity, even stupidity. His straight arrow reputation took a hit over close ties to a failed Arizona banker in the 1980s, from whom McCain accepted Caribbean holidays and free flights. This gambling streak, it could be said, went all the way back to Annapolis, where he put his graduation and future military career at risk over a television set.

"He loved to watch *Maverick,* the James Garner television series on Sunday nights," explained Frank Gamboa, who at

McCain's instigation, chipped in to buy a television and conceal it on campus. Having a television was against Academy rules, and when the Company Officer discovered it, he requested a single name to take the heavy load of the demerits. "We used to make every decision by rock, paper and scissors," said Gamboa, noting that the other four students in the ownership circle did not want John McCain to participate in the gamble. If he lost, midshipman McCain would exceed the permitted limit for demerits and would almost certainly be expelled from the Academy. "He insisted on participating," Gamboa recalled. "But McCain was in luck. Fortunately, it fell to one of the others who had no demerits."

In 1958, John McCain graduated fifth from the bottom of his class. According to tradition, President Eisenhower shook hands with the graduates who had excelled and offered his commiserations to the "anchorman". That's the midshipman who comes in at the very bottom of the class. "I wish I had done a bit worse, so I could have met the President," McCain commented on the campaign trail, when asked about his poor academic performance.

Fifty years on, the regimen at the Naval Academy has not changed much from John McCain's day. Demerits still apply, and often before sunrise you can hear the men, and women now too, performing their early morning drills. Midshipmen do not have to scale the wall to escape the drudgery of studying these days, because leisure time is built into their schedule. As of 2008, however, one thing remained the same. There was still a McCain enrolled at Annapolis. John McCain's son Jack was to graduate in 2009, making four generations of naval officers in the family.

Senator McCain's penchant for flying by the seat of his pants was the basis for many of the personal stories that surfaced during the 2008 election campaign. Shortly after graduation, his failure to prepare for a flight test almost cost him his life when his plane went down and quickly sank in Corpus Christi Bay off the Texas coast.

"He was sitting on the bottom of the aircraft, and he said, 'You know, I remember there's some kind of switch here somewhere that blows the canopy off the airplane, but I didn't read the book – and I don't know where the switch is. So I guess I'm dead'," Admiral Chuck Larson, another classmate, recounted to CNN.

These daredevil tales were in sharp contrast to the almost studied caution Barack Obama adhered to on his journey towards Washington. Since arriving in Chicago in the mid-1980s to work as a community organiser, Obama was known mainly as a workaholic brimming with ambition. But apart from his personal admission that he had smoked marijuana and had done a bit of "blow" in his teenage years, Barack Obama's stories of misspent youth could not match John McCain's love of risk-taking, mischief-making and partying with pretty women.

In 1965, John McCain married Carol Shepp, a dark-haired model from Philadelphia. Shepp had two sons from a previous marriage, and together she and McCain had a daughter. But it was not long before McCain was dodging death again. In 1967, while serving on board the *USS Forrestall* in the Gulf of Tonkin during the Vietnam War, a freak accident prompted a chain reaction of explosions on the deck of the carrier engulfing 134 servicemen. McCain, who was sitting in his plane, miraculously climbed out and walked down its nose to safety. But later that year, on a bombing mission over North Vietnam,

John McCain's luck ran out. His plane was shot down. As he frantically tried to eject, his body hit against the side of the plane, and he broke both arms as well as his right knee. McCain landed in a shallow lake in the middle of Hanoi and was immediately taken prisoner by the Vietnamese. He was thirty years old and had a baby daughter at home. He would not see his family for five years.

"I was brought in through enormous steel gates, above which was painted the legend 'Maison Centrale'," McCain wrote in *Faith of My Fathers*. "I had been shot down a short walk's distance from the French-built prison Hoa Lo, which the POW's had named 'The Hanoi Hilton'. As the massive steel doors loudly clanked shut behind me, I felt a deeper dread than I have ever felt since."

For the next five years, McCain and other POWs captured by the North Vietnamese were shuffled back and forth between the Hoa Lo prison and more remote detention camps where their days were spent in fear and isolation. "Not unlike flying supersonic jets, hours and hours of boredom frequently interrupted with moments of stark terror," is how seventy-two-year-old Orson Swindle remembers their time in captivity. Swindle, a Marine Officer from Georgia who was shot down in November 1966, knew of the McCain family and had heard that John was in the same prison about a year before he made contact.

"Our first communication was tapping through walls," Swindle said, explaining that tapping was the code developed in flight school to help the men keep track of one another if taken prisoner. Sleep deprivation, beatings and being suspended from a ceiling by your thumbs were among the methods the Vietnamese used to try to force confessions from their captives. John McCain described having his arms pulled behind his back to the point where his shoulders almost dislocated. "We did everything we could to support each other. When a guy would be tossed back in his cell completely defeated, tortured and in great pain, we'd tap through the wall, 'Hang in there. Good night. God bless. We'll talk to you tomorrow,' Swindle recalled. "The next day we might be the ones getting the treatment."

In 1971, Swindle and McCain shared a prison cell. By then the worst of the torture appeared to be over, and John McCain had made a life-altering decision. A year earlier, despite physical injuries which worsened due to a lack of medical attention, McCain had refused an offer of early release from his Vietnamese captors. His status as the son of an American admiral, he felt, might be too useful to the enemy.

"If I went home, they would use it as propaganda to demoralise my fellow prisoners," McCain told Republican supporters in St Paul, Minnesota, in September 2008. "Our Code said we could only go home in the order of our capture, and there were men who had been shot down before me. I thought about it though. I wasn't in great shape, and I missed everything about America. But I turned it down."

As a result, the Navy pilot remained in his prison cell for three more years. During those years it took all McCain's mental courage to maintain morale in the face of loneliness and mind-numbing boredom. "John is a voracious reader," said Swindle, who recalled that he and McCain developed a course for other POWs on the history of the English and American novel. "We went back to Daniel Defoe and *Robinson Crusoe* and *Moll Flanders*, and worked our way up through Hemingway and Sinclair Lewis and F. Scott Fitzgerald. We explained how the novel evolved from those long wordy things we all read at school to the more entertaining versions," remembered Swindle, who now lives in Virginia.

To pass the years, John McCain told stories to his fellow prisoners which he called "Monday Night at the Movies", and the men fashioned playing cards out of the crude toilet paper the Vietnamese prison guards gave them. Using cigarette ashes and dirt, they made ink to mark the cards. "To shuffle the cards was quite an endeavour since the paper was rather flimsy," Swindle told me.

"Do you ever have bad dreams about those days in captivity?" I asked Swindle, who was held prisoner for six years. "No," he replied, claiming that the experience had given the men a life-long bond and strengthened their will to serve America. In the years that followed, about two dozen of the POWs reached the rank of General or Admiral or became doctors or lawyers.

In 1973, McCain, Swindle and their fellow POWs stepped off airplanes back onto American soil. They returned to a country deeply divided over the Vietnam War, which had claimed the lives of 58,000 Americans. To many, the POWs were the only heroes of that war. But, after five or six years away, home life had changed too. Some of the prisoners' wives had remarried, not knowing if their husbands would ever return, and loved ones had died. The cost of everything had doubled, and an Opel GT was just one of many new cars cruising along the American roads.

John McCain's bones had never been set properly in captivity, and he returned in bad physical shape. "He wanted to return to flying, but he had a damaged right knee, which was frozen straight out because of the fractures he received when he ejected," said Diane Lawrence, who first met McCain when he came to her as a patient seeking physical rehabilitation. "In order to pass his flight physical, he had to be able to flex his right knee to 90 degrees." Diane worked on it twice a week for nine months, and by increments McCain made progress. "He would take the pain as long as he could and then he would say, 'That's it'," Diane Lawrence recalled from her home in Maryland. McCain did pass his physical and was cleared to fly again. He invited Diane to dinner to meet another of the recently released prisoners of war, Bill Lawrence. "We married on the 29th of August 1974, on John's birthday," Diane said, adding that John McCain remained a life-long friend even after Vice Admiral Bill Lawrence's death in 2005.

But by 1979 McCain's own family life had begun to come apart, mainly because he had set his cap at someone new. At a party in Honolulu, Hawaii, a twenty-five-year-old from Arizona had caught his eye. Her name was Cindy Hensley. In his book *Worth the Fighting For*, McCain described their first meeting: "She was lovely, intelligent and charming, seventeen years my junior but poised and confident. I monopolised her attention the entire time, taking care to prevent anyone else from intruding on our conversation. When it came time to leave the party, I persuaded her to join me for drinks at the Royal Hawaiian Hotel. By the evening's end I was in love." Hensley's father owned a multi-million dollar beer distributorship in Arizona. In 1980, John McCain and Carol Shepp divorced. A month later, Cindy Hensley became Cindy McCain.

Since 1977, Captain John McCain had worked on Capitol Hill as a liaison between the Navy and members of Congress and had developed a taste for politics. With the help of Cindy's family connections, he decided to move west and run for Congress in Arizona. John Sydney McCain III had made the rank of Navy Captain, but unlike his father Jack and his grandfather Slew he would not become an Admiral. John McCain would move up the ladder on a new track. Orson Swindle, who helped John McCain campaign for the presidency, said he was not surprised to learn in 1983 that his old cellmate from the "Hanoi Hilton" was heading into the political arena. "When you sit in jail waiting on a political decision to either win a war or quit, it's frustrating. We all said, 'By God, when we get home, we are never going to take our freedom and the way this government works for granted. We are going to be involved. We are going to make a difference'."

Four years after entering Congress, Arizona Representative John McCain advanced to the upper house and became Senator McCain. Fourteen years later in 2000, he made his first run for president but lost in the primaries to George W. Bush. In 2008, however, the "Maverick" had seen off a host of challengers to take the Republican nomination. Though 2008 would be a tough year for a Republican candidate, many felt that, with his personal story of heroism and love of country, John McCain might just be the one Republican who could make it to the White House.

TOWARDS THE END OF MCCAIN'S FIRST Senate term in 1992, Barack Obama arrived back in Chicago from Boston's Harvard Law School with politics on his mind. He had held the school's highest student position, president of the *Harvard Law Review*, having been the first African-American to do so in the school's 104-year history. The only other elected office anyone had heard Obama express any interest in was mayor of Chicago. City Hall had the power to decide who got what in the vast

Midwestern city, and an African-American named Harold Washington had been its mayor in the 1980s. "The path of Harold Washington became a model in the mind of Obama," said Mike Kruglik, who had briefly talked politics with Obama before he left for Harvard. Harold Washington had a law degree and had become a state legislator before running for mayor. "He inspired Obama," Kruglik claimed. But the mayoral office was unavailable. Richard M. Daley, of the famed Irish Daley family, had manoeuvred his way into City Hall, and his knowledge of Chicago's urban politics was likely to keep him there for a long time.

Having been absent for four years, Barack Obama was disheartened by what he saw when he returned to Chicago. "I would find the signs of decay accelerated throughout the South Side – the neighbourhoods shabbier, the children edgier and less restrained, the jails bursting with glowering youth, my brothers without prospects," he wrote in *Dreams from My Father*.

The first job Obama took was running a voter registration drive, something that would be useful when he battled for the presidency in 2008. Registering new voters, especially those who will vote for you, is one of the smartest strategies around. The Obama campaign registered hundreds of thousands of new voters in each battleground state, including many African-Americans and young people.

Barack Obama's entry into politics via his 1996 election to the Illinois General Assembly was remarkable only in that he knocked his female opponent off the ballot by challenging the validity of her petition's signatures. Obama ran as an independent Democrat on the city's South Side, where the University of Chicago is located and where his Harvard education was advantageous. He also took a job teaching at the University's Law School, where he was viewed as a liberal intellectual.

At the General Assembly in Springfield, Illinois, Barack Obama was like a fish out of water. A constitutional law lecturer who liked the sound his own voice, the newcomer was routinely mocked and heckled by the hardboiled politicos who ran the state. Shortly after his arrival at the state capital, he told friends he was "getting it from all sides". Political colleagues reported that the power-hungry rookie let it be known from day one that there were "higher places he wanted to be".

Obama quickly learned the ropes. He made friends with the power players, joined committees and attached his name to as many legislative bills as possible. He worked to establish a state-funded screening programme for prostate cancer, a disease that disproportionately affects African-Americans. Obama also increased funds for after-school programmes in Illinois and accelerated the investigation of rampant abuses in the state's nursing homes.

But Barack Obama's first big political test came in 2000, when he tried to make it to Washington DC by challenging a black Chicago congressman for his seat. Representative Bobby Rush, however, had deep roots in Chicago's black community and would not be easily moved aside by Obama, who had made his home in the city's elite Hyde Park neighbourhood. Rush defended his turf easily, and Obama emerged from the experience licking his wounds. "He made an extreme misjudgment in entering that race," said Don Rose, a retired political consultant in Chicago. Obama's own assessment of the experience was that he had got "spanked". His political career seemed to have stalled at the state level.

As a husband and father of two young girls, Obama had career decisions to make. Back in 1992, he had married girlfriend Michelle Robinson, whom he met in 1989 at a Chicago law firm. Michelle, a talented graduate of both Princeton and Harvard, had been assigned to mentor Obama when he arrived as a summer intern. Instead of submitting to her mentoring, Obama just pestered Robinson to go on dates with him. She thought dating someone in the office was "tacky" but now claims his offer to buy her ice cream after the company picnic was what closed the deal! "Barack didn't pledge riches, only a life that would be interesting," Michelle Obama told ABC television in 2008 of his promise to her before they married. "On that, he has delivered," she said.

Michelle Obama remained largely uninvolved in her husband's early political career and would have been happier to have him around the house more regularly. During his time as a member of the Illinois General Assembly, Barack Obama lived in a hotel in Springfield during the week, while his wife worked back home in Chicago and cared for daughters Malia and Sasha. But following his loss to Bobby Rush, Obama decided to set his political sights even higher. He would run for the US Senate in 2004. Advisers counselled against it, putting his chances of making it to Washington DC at no more than one in three. But according to journalist David Mendell, who covered the 2004 Senate race for the *Chicago Tribune*, Obama saw it differently: "He felt if he could get liberals and blacks and marry those two constituencies together – and maybe get a few votes downstate in Illinois – he could prevail." Another factor in going ahead with the 2004 race, thought Mendell, was that Obama managed to convince Michelle that it was the smart thing to do.

Michelle Obama introduced her husband to Marty Nesbitt, an African-American who played basketball with her brother Craig Robinson. Nesbitt worked for Penny Pritzker, the heiress to the Hyatt Hotel chain. Since Obama needed to raise about $10 million to run a state-wide campaign, a meeting was arranged at the Pritzker cottage in Michigan. Obama made his case. "He sold himself to her on this weekend. She thought that African-Americans needed more representation in Washington and black men in particular," said David Mendell. Not only did Pritzker donate to Obama's campaign, she had access to a web of other donors who also contributed.

On the political front, Obama had nurtured another important connection – Emil Jones Junior, Chairman of the Illinois State Senate. Jones, one of the most senior black politicians in Illinois, initially regarded Obama with suspicion. But over time the older man warmed to the young legislator and became something of a political mentor to Obama. "When he decided to run for the US Senate, he [Jones] lined up a lot of black committee men to support Obama," Don Rose said. "This was very important in unifying the black base for Obama." The candidate was also blessed with a mountain of good luck, in that several of his rivals for the Senate seat became tangled up in personal scandals that left them either badly damaged or unelectable.

Another key player who joined the Obama electoral effort at this time was David Axelrod, a former *Chicago Tribune* journalist who had forged a successful career running political campaigns. As a strategist, Axelrod was known for his ability to sell candidates to voters through the use of masterful television advertising campaigns. With people like David Axelrod and Penny Pritzker on his team, Barack Obama became the candidate to beat. The only thing he had not done was kick his addiction to cigarettes, a personal weakness Obama tried to hide from reporters on the 2004 Senate campaign trail. "The caravan would be rolling through the cornfields of Illinois, and all of a sudden we'd all pull over at a gas station. For a while I thought he was drinking too much water," recalled David Mendell. "But he was going in there to get his nicotine fix. His wife had been trying forever to get him to stop smoking." According to Mendell, Obama's later decision to quit smoking was part of Michelle Obama's 2006 agreement to support her husband's audacious bid for the presidency of the United States. "I'll go along with your presidential race if you quit," Mrs Obama told her husband.

But with the 2004 Senate race still to be won, Barack Obama received another lucky break. His invitation to address Boston's August 2004 Democratic Convention brought him national exposure. In the middle of an election campaign, the coverage was worth more than any advertising a candidate could hope to buy. Obama had struck a chord as a symbol of hope and unity at a time when America was demoralised and divided over the war in Iraq. As Barack Obama strode into Boston's Fleet Centre on the evening before his groundbreaking speech, he threw a quick comment back to journalist David Mendell who was trailing just behind. "I'm LeBron, baby," Obama said, referring to the star American basketball player LeBron James. "I've got some game. I can play at this level."

9

Drill, Baby, Drill

"The only thing I've heard him [Obama] say is that we should inflate our tires. So he has no plan for addressing the energy challenges that we face." – JOHN MCCAIN

I WAS ON A VISIT BACK TO IRELAND WHEN THE two-horse race got underway in the summer of 2008. Just as in America, those following the election in Ireland were split on whether Barack Obama's caravan of hope and change could really make it all the way to 1600 Pennsylvania Avenue. Despite Ireland being in a decisive "No" mood – having rejected the Lisbon Treaty – the view from home was that while the US needed a shake-up of its own, Americans were probably not ready to take the radical step of electing a black man to the presidency.

"McCain will win it," was the prediction of those acquainted with America's more conservative streak. Returned emigrants I met while touring with my American husband and mother-in-law delivered their political forecast with the wisdom of those who had seen the blatant segregation that still exists in American cities. I wondered, however, if behind this doubt there was also a sense of distrust in America still lingering from the transatlantic divisions over the Iraq war. "They'd have a terrible time keeping him alive," one woman remarked, guessing that, as president, Obama would not survive more than a year in America. This fear was commonplace across Ireland, despite the fact that Barack Obama had won the Democratic nomination by more votes than any other candidate in history and was continuing to raise more money from ordinary Americans than anyone had ever thought possible.

"They will try to scare you by saying he's different, that he's got a funny name, and he doesn't look like the other presidents on the dollar bills," Obama declared at a rally in Missouri in the heat of the summer, leaping headfirst into the debate over race. Republicans had superimposed Barack Obama's face on a one dollar bill in an advertisement questioning if too much change would be a good thing for America. Most Americans had to search the internet to find the ad, but Republicans claimed Obama had overreacted by making it about race when it was not meant that way.

"I think Obama's inexperience is more of an issue than the color of his skin," Republican strategist Joe Watkins suggested at the height of the dollar bill spat. Watkins, himself an African-American, claimed that while some people might vote on race, he did not believe it would decide the election. "For Americans, race is not the thing that keeps them voting for a person as much as it is issues and who the person is," Watkins argued. Retired political consultant Don Rose disagreed, believing that racial prejudice was the reason Obama was running just four points ahead of John McCain all summer – while Democrats in general were running a full ten points ahead of Republicans. "Part of the gap is pure race," Rose said. "He's unlikely to overcome all that."

Part of this "race gap" I encountered in Kentucky and throughout the Midwest, and even in my own adopted hometown of Annapolis. "Let them have their black president for four years and get it over with," a neighbour commented to me as we chatted one evening. "Then we can move on." The election, I found, roused strong feelings in people that had otherwise remained hidden.

In swing states like Pennsylvania and Ohio, Barack Obama also had cause to worry. As late as August 2008, with just eight weeks to the election, Cleveland real estate broker John Lynch remained sceptical that Obama could garner enough support among blue-collar white voters in Ohio. He just could not see a majority of them electing a black president.

Since I am Irish and a child of the seventies and eighties, these "blue-collar whites" reminded me of the old Daz washing powder ads on RTÉ which claimed your clothes got so white they were blue! Here, too, it seemed the blue whites were the whitest of them all and the least likely to vote for a black man. An acquaintance who had visited a firing range in Pennsylvania, a largely blue-collar state, had reported back that some of the shooters at the range took their target practice on images of Barack Obama. At least two poorly formulated plots to assassinate Obama were foiled in the summer of 2008.

Aside from the race gap, the candidates' histories and experiences also benefited John McCain in the early summer of 2008, bolstering his chances when he should have been struggling to make the case for a third Republican term. Older Americans equated McCain's age with wisdom. They admired his military service and long years in the Senate. Obama's few years as a Chicago community organiser and puny legislative history in the Illinois Senate did not inspire confidence.

John McCain, at seventy-two years of age, had a world view which was understandably closer to that of older Americans. His desire for victory in Iraq, many believed, would strengthen US influence abroad. Voters who had lived through the bruising Vietnam defeat feared that leaving Iraq too soon could be seen as another weak retreat. Finally, older Americans believed that "change" should be brought about slowly and deliberately – by leaders with a long view of history and not at the behest of hoards of text-messaging youths.

"The young must earn their dues," I heard more than a few times, meaning that Obama and his supporters should fold their tents and return in a few years. Even those who shared concerns about John McCain's age initially seemed willing to elect him for four years as a "holding president" rather than take a chance on the younger man. A *Newsweek* poll at the start of the presidential election found that 55 per cent of Americans considered that electing Barack Obama would be the bigger risk. Just 35 per cent felt they would be taking a big risk by electing John McCain.

Of course, almost 18 million Democrats had already taken a chance by nominating Barack Obama over the better-known Hillary Clinton. But primary voters represent just a small cross-section of Americans and tend to be drawn from the extremes of the political parties – the diehard Democrats and Republicans. The November elections are about attracting the larger middle ground, including the growing number of independents who swing between parties from one election to the next. Obama could already count on African-Americans, a majority of Hispanics and young college-educated voters. Those he needed to bring on board were grandparents, middle-class voters and those "Daz blue whites".

The first thing Team Obama did after securing the Democratic nomination in June was to move the Democratic National Committee headquarters to Chicago. The Midwest's "Windy City" is Obama's adopted hometown. It's where he started out as a community organiser, where he met and married his wife Michelle, and where he entered the world of politics as a state assemblyman and later as a US senator representing Illinois. Though Chicago politics is synonymous with powerful machines and corruption, moving the party's election committee westwards telegraphed a message to the Washington establishment that the Obama campaign would continue to approach the 2008 race from the vantage point of an outsider.

Without giving Hillary Clinton time to draw breath after her exit from the race, Barack Obama recruited her former campaign manager. Patti Solis Doyle had been jettisoned back in February after Clinton failed to take a commanding lead on Super Tuesday. The fact that she was now joining Obama, specifically to work with his future vice-presidential pick, was the first loud signal that Obama was not considering Clinton as his running mate. This was a blow to the majority of Democrats who still believed Clinton would be the obvious best choice for vice-president.

"Less than a one per cent chance," was how one Clinton insider put it to me in the weeks after Hillary had suspended her campaign. Barack Obama was coy. "She would be on anyone's shortlist," he would say whenever asked about the possibility of Hillary joining his ticket. But in a widely reported conversation with a reporter in July, Obama let slip one key reason that seemingly explained why Clinton's chances were so slim – Bill. Obama's advisers still worried he would be taking on two

Clintons, Bill and Hillary, at a time when Obama was trying to put his own stamp of leadership on the Democratic Party.

By late July 2008, news was circulating that Hillary Clinton would speak on the Tuesday night of the Democratic convention to be held the following month in Denver. Since the vice-presidential candidate is traditionally introduced on Wednesday of convention week, this was further proof to Clinton's supporters that Hillary was off Obama's list. New names began to surface, including Virginia Governor Tim Kaine and Indiana Senator Evan Bayh. Another woman, Kansas Governor Kathleen Sebelius, was also considered. Barack Obama insisted publicly that he needed both Clintons campaigning for him, but he had yet to arrange a face to face meeting with Bill Clinton. The two men did not meet until 11 September 2008, nearly two months before the election. While Hillary continued to make public appearances and campaign stops for Obama, Bill Clinton spent the summer out of sight. Reports of his humour were all strikingly similar. He was "in a funk" over the failure of Hillary's campaign.

Long before Obama became the Democratic nominee, his backroom team was working on a national strategy to beat John McCain. Early on, it was clear that they were setting their sights much higher than John Kerry had done in 2004 or Al Gore in 2000. Rather than submitting to the usual limitations of the Electoral College by focusing on a just a handful of battleground states, the Obama team rolled out what it called its "Fifty State Strategy". It would fight for a victory across the entire map, even in states where both history and conventional wisdom dictated Obama had little chance of winning. "We are not basing victory on Karl Rove's Red State–Blue State politics of division," the Democratic National Committee announced in an email on

20 June 2008. "We are not focusing all our resources on the so-called 'swing states', but are working in every state."

This was a bold move away from the accepted wisdom that the route to victory in November was to hold on to those states that John Kerry had won in 2004 and to add one or two more. An alternative formula promoted by pollsters was to win two of the three big states – Ohio, Pennsylvania and Florida – that had proved crucial to George W. Bush's victories in 2000 and 2004. Bush had won both Florida and Ohio in 2004, but neither state would be easily flipped over to the Democratic side. Instead of confining itself to such narrow options, the Obama team opened up the playing field to include a range of states – Colorado, Virginia, North Carolina, Indiana, Montana and even Alaska – which it believed could be switched from Red to Blue. This larger playing field would provide multiple paths to the 270 electoral votes needed to win the presidency on 4 November. Taking note, John McCain began to target states like Michigan, Minnesota, New Hampshire and Pennsylvania, which he felt he could take from the Democrats.

The second element of Obama's national strategy was to out-fundraise and outspend his opponent so that John McCain would have to use money where he did not plan to. To set this up, Barack Obama made his first major policy u-turn. He had always promised that if he became the Democratic nominee, he would stick with public financing for the November election. By late June, however, Obama had figured out that he could raise much more cash on his own, so he backed out. "To change his position was a big disappointment to a lot of his supporters, not just a flip-flop for Republicans to talk about," said Republican strategist Joe Watkins, "especially after he had been so passionate about public financing." For a week, Obama was tagged as a hypocrite, even by his own supporters, but his move was seen ultimately as part and parcel of the battle that goes on every four years for the White House.

Public financing came into being in 1976 as a way to clean up the way money is raised for elections. When Americans fill out their annual tax form, they are asked to tick a box if they wish to individually contribute $4 to the public financing system. The total collected is then divided equally between the two parties' nominees for the next presidential election. By agreeing to take public financing, a candidate forfeits the right to raise money independently during certain periods of the electoral process. In 2008, public financing would have provided Barack Obama and John McCain with $85 million each for the final two months of the campaign – almost $1.5 million a day. Towards the end of the election, however, Obama raised over $4 million a day from supporters, and in September 2008 alone, he managed to take in an incredible $150 million.

In anticipation of a record cash haul, Obama's team poured money into television advertisements in eighteen targeted states, including Georgia, Indiana, Wisconsin, Ohio and Florida. For Obama to win in the southern Republican state of Georgia would be difficult, but the Democrat's strategy forced John McCain to use up his funds defending a state previously considered to be safe McCain territory. Obama's decision to compete early and hard in several Republican states would pay huge dividends later on.

As the presidential race progressed, the make-up of the campaigns also continued to take shape. With Obama's operation headquartered in Chicago, several in his inner circle were old friends from the city. Most had come on board four years earlier for his US Senate race and have remained in his inner circle. As his national fundraising chairperson, Obama chose Penny Pritzker, the Hyatt hotel heiress, whom he had convinced to back him in 2004. Other prominent business people in Obama's support group included James Crown, son of Chicago billionaire Lester Crown, and African-American tycoon Marty Nesbitt, who had initially put Obama in touch with Pritzker. Obama also kept close to him Valerie Jarrett – a long-time family friend who acted as a personal adviser.

The most visible team member was Obama's chief strategist David Axelrod, a native New Yorker who had spent the past 30 years navigating Chicago urban politics, as well as running campaigns for Hillary Clinton and John Edwards. Axelrod had lost several previous presidential campaigns but was intent on breaking his losing streak with Barack Obama. Commenting on his decision to join Obama's 2004 Senate campaign, Axelrod had said, "I thought if I could help Barack Obama get to Washington, I would have accomplished something great in my life". The sad-eyed, mustachioed fifty-three-year-old regularly spoke on Obama's behalf, seeking to tamp down emerging controversies, and appeared almost too mild-mannered for such a dog-eat-dog business. According to Don Rose, however, David Axelrod has a real edge to him. "He's quite capable of reaching Rovian levels of nastiness wherever he thinks it's appropriate," Rose said, adding that some of Obama's punchiest lines on the stump bore the Axelrod hallmark.

What gave the Obama team its apparent group harmony, according to Don Rose, was that both David Axelrod and campaign manager David Plouffe had built a company together, AKP&D Message and Media, and were never pulling against one another. "They may have differing ideas, but they do not compete," Rose explained. "When an idea is adopted, no one dissents. They know if they do, they would be out, because this is a very tightly knit working organisation." Together with "No Drama Obama", Axelrod and Plouffe managed to keep their disagreements private and under the media radar. When they did disagree it was over how hard they should hit John McCain. Barack Obama, wishing to run a dignified campaign, constantly argued against negative advertising – even as some of his staff urged him to aggressively attack his opponent.

The next layers of activity in a presidential campaign structure are the special advisers. In Obama's case, these ran into the hundreds. The foreign policy section alone consisted of a core group of seven to ten people led by Anthony Lake and Susan Rice, both of whom had served in Bill Clinton's administration. Underneath them were special groups dealing with Asia, Europe, international energy, the UN and nuclear non-proliferation. Each group had about thirty people feeding into it. In total, over 300 experts, including former ambassadors, former government advisers and academics, kept Barack Obama up to date on foreign policy.

Irish issues came under the Europe heading. On a day-to-day basis, Ireland was not a top priority for Anthony Lake during the campaign. "But it would be on his radar screen. He would know who all the players were," one group member said. An early omission by the Obama team to include an envoy to Northern Ireland in the party platform was later corrected, so that both candidates were promising to continue the practice started during the Clinton years. Obama also announced a team of high-profile legislators to advise him on Irish issues, including the former Northern Ireland peace talks co-chair George Mitchell, Senators Pat Leahy and Chris Dodd, and Maryland Governor Martin O'Malley. "I am delighted to be able to call upon a 'Dream Team' who cherish the US-Irish bond as I do." Obama said.

The final part of the Obama offensive was its communications strategy aimed not just at the grassroots but the internet-based "netroots". The campaign, for example, had launched its social networking site, MyBarackObama.com, designed along the same lines as Facebook or MySpace. Twenty-seven-year-old Chris Hughes, one of Facebook's founders, helped to shape it as a cyberspace hub where supporters could meet up to talk politics, organise fundraisers, set up home-based phone banks and even find dates. The Obama campaign also created a special YouTube channel where supporters posted their own videos and raised funds. While both teams harnessed the power of the internet, Obama's online traffic throughout the election was double that of John McCain's.

IN JULY 2008 JOHN MCCAIN SHOOK up his core team for the second time since entering the race. "It's a very loose structure," an insider divulged to me at the time, frustrated that the message tended to shift with McCain's mood. The latest response was to draft Steve Schmidt, who had helped re-elect President Bush to a second term in 2004.

Schmidt, a tough, thirty-seven-year-old Republican operative, was often described as a protégé of Karl Rove, President Bush's chief strategist. In 2007, Rove had resigned under a cloud of allegations and a flurry of subpoenas concerning the Justice Department's firing of federal attorneys in which he played a part. During the 2008 campaign, however, Karl Rove continued to dispense advice to all of the candidates from the studios of Fox News where he had become a regular pundit.

As a message manager, Schmidt ran the "rapid response" media operation for George Bush's 2004 election. He was a "war room" operative charged with putting out instant rebuttals to missives from John Kerry's side. He was also credited with working a near miracle for Arnold Schwarzenegger, guiding him to a second-term victory as governor of California despite dismal approval ratings. Now Schmidt and campaign manager Rick Davis were expected to work magic for John McCain, and they decided to accomplish this by making the 2008 race largely about Barack Obama.

In a year that heavily favoured Democrats, Republican strategists figured that the one way they might still be able to win was to raise serious questions about Obama's readiness for office. Casting doubt on his abilities to lead in a major crisis could easily drive voters into the arms of the more experienced war hero McCain. It was either that or a terrorist attack, which nobody wanted to imagine, though at least one senior McCain adviser was willing to talk about. "It would be an advantage," Charlie Black admitted to *Forbes Magazine* when asked how a surprise attack might play for the Republicans in 2008.

I had also heard the "only a terrorist attack" line from other Republicans, who felt George Bush's legacy would doom them to certain defeat. Yet as the weeks dragged on and polls remained close, it became clear that, while Americans were fed up with Republican rule, they were not yet comfortable with Barack Obama. After all the packed stadiums and the yearning for change, the presidential contest did not look like being a cakewalk for the Democrat.

THE MAIN PHASE OF THE CAMPAIGN began with Barack Obama trying to paint John McCain as George Bush III and McCain attempting to tag Obama as a rookie not yet ready for prime time. Obama then contrived to connect McCain to Washington DC lobbyists, several of whom were on the Republican's advisory team, but McCain countered by pinning the "celebrity" label on Obama. Amid all the noise, it was not shaping up as an election that would be fought on the issues – despite the fact that John McCain and Barack Obama stood poles apart on some of the biggest problems ever facing America.

To be or not to be in Iraq was the thorniest question. After seven years at war, the US was spending $10 billion a month trying to stabilise Iraq while fighting a resurgent Taliban and foreign fighters in Afghanistan. Barack Obama, who had opposed the Iraq war, planned to bring US troops home within the first sixteen months of his presidency, but John McCain saw no sense in withdrawing troops until they could come home "victorious". Having initially speculated that America could stay in Iraq "for one hundred years", McCain quickly agreed – having been blasted from all sides – that as president he would take another look at the situation in 2013.

As the economy began to splutter, both candidates reacted slowly. Their intention was to stick to competing philosophies – "I am my brother's keeper" for Democrats, who believe government has a role to help those who can't help themselves, and "You're on Your Own" or "YOYO" for Republicans. McCain planned to keep George Bush's tax cuts for the richest corporations on the premise that "trickle down" wealth is the foundation of job creation. Obama planned to raise corporate taxes and give everyone else a break. But this was before the Wall Street meltdown brought America unprecedented bailouts, nationalised banks and "Joe the Plumber".

The candidates stood apart on the culture wars, too, appealing to opposite sides. Barack Obama, who is pro-choice, stated that he was against any reversal of *Roe* v. *Wade*, the 1972 Supreme Court decision permitting abortion. John McCain, a staunch pro-life advocate, would not interfere with existing law but was more likely to appoint conservative justices who might make changes. Of the nine Supreme Court justices, who in 2008 were evenly balanced with one swing voter in the middle, three liberals might retire or die in the next presidential term. Under a McCain presidency, replacing any of them with a conservative justice was sure to tip the balance so as to change abortion law as well as a range of personal privacy laws. Barack Obama, however, would likely replace the justices with new liberals and maintain the Supreme Court's balance.

But of all issues facing America in 2008, the one that caught fire in the early part of the Presidential election was not Iraq, or the ticking time bomb beneath the sub-prime mortgage crisis, or the almost bankrupt Social Security system, or the forty-five million Americans without any health insurance. It was the price of petrol. Like no other problem, the summer's increase in price from $3 to over $4 a gallon panicked everyone.

"I'm driving around in circles like I used to do during the nineteen seventies' oil shock," a co-volunteer at the St Vincent de Paul in Annapolis told me – explaining how these days she maps out the shops she needs to go to and drives from one to the other in a single trip, rather than shopping several times a week.

America is the world's third-largest oil producer and sources roughly a third of its needs at home. The rest of the twenty million barrels it gulps down daily comes from places like Canada, Saudi Arabia, Venezuela and Mexico. By a long shot, America has always been the world's largest oil consumer, though, with four times the US population, China is catching up. This increased Chinese demand, plus market speculation, and reduced output from Iraq owing to the war were among the factors that drove oil from around $25 in 2002 to a record high of $147 a barrel in July 2008.

The effect of $4 a gallon gas was immediate. In Baltimore early-morning bus routes quickly filled up, workers tried to switch to four-day weeks, and in extreme cases people pawned watches and rings – just so they could fill the tank. SUVs sat idle in car dealerships, and waiting-lists for hybrid cars grew longer. Scooters, bikes, Segways and – God forbid – walkers took to the streets! From November 2007 to June 2008, Americans drove 5.3 billion fewer miles than in the same period the previous year.

John McCain was the first to call for drilling off the US coast as a way to end America's dependency on foreign oil. Having danced with the environmentalists and initially opposed drilling, McCain quickly noticed that Americans liked the idea of finding their own energy supply. Calling it a "national mission to eliminate our dependence on foreign oil," McCain demanded an end to a moratorium on domestic oil drilling and ecstatic crowds at his rallies responded with chants of "Drill, Baby, Drill!" Their chanting was sweet music to President Bush's ears. For eight years, Bush had been a cheerleader for drilling but until the gas pumps started showing $4 a gallon, Democrats and conservationists had held Bush back.

As an environmentalist, Barack Obama was in a more difficult position. He had received the endorsement of Al Gore, Nobel Prize winner and chief go-to guy on all things green. Obama called for carbon emissions to be reduced by a whopping 80 per cent by 2050, and rejected offshore drilling as an environmental gamble that would take decades to produce oil. To ease the pain at the pumps, Obama called for new powers to prevent market speculators from jacking up the price of oil, and he vowed to impose greater fuel efficiency standards on Ford, GM and the other American car manufacturers. Then, like a father dispensing unsolicited advice to his children, Obama suggested that if motorists rotated their tires regularly and kept them properly inflated, they would "save all the oil that they're talking about getting out of drilling".

John McCain's people handed tire gauges out to the media marked with the slogan "Obama's Energy Plan". They mocked him and called him "Dr No". Republicans accused Obama of being against offshore drilling, nuclear power, nuclear reprocessing, and even waste storage at Yucca Mountain, a cavern dug deep into the Nevada desert. When I visited Yucca in 2003, the huge facility was almost ready to go, but America's only repository for nuclear waste became mired in controversy and has never been used.

"The only thing I've heard him say is that we should inflate our tires. So he has no plan for addressing the energy challenges that we face," McCain declared as the energy debate reached its height. Senator McCain had said "No" several times to green legislation providing tax incentives for wind and solar energy, but it did not seem to matter. We were in the hot steamy days of summer, and the average American began to realise he was lining the pockets of Saudi princes, Hugo Chavez and other foreign leaders who did not like America very much. For a while, it looked as though the candidate with the biggest oil drill might become the next president.

10

"More Better Than Bush"

"People of Berlin, people of the world.... The walls between races and tribes, natives and immigrants, Christian and Muslim and Jew cannot stand." – BARACK OBAMA

BY LATE JULY OF 2008 PRESIDENT George W. Bush had faded into the background of day-to-day politics. With banks collapsing and American homes being repossessed at a rate of 8,000 a week, he probably felt it wise to keep a low profile and start packing for home in Crawford, Texas. The President was no longer part of the twenty-four-hour news cycle, and the further he remained from public view, the better it suited the Republican presidential nominee John McCain. Network television cameras permanently stationed on the White House lawn shut off their lights, and members of the press corps – fearing they might go rigid with boredom – fled to the campaign trail.

It was little wonder then, when Barack Obama departed for the Middle East and Europe on a chartered plane complete with an entourage of aides and advisers, that everyone mistook him for America's top political figure. Obama rubbed shoulders with German Chancellor Angela Merkel, French President

Nicolas Sarkozy, Britain's Gordon Brown and Iraqi Prime Minister Nouri al-Maliki, all of whom treated him more like a visiting head of state than a candidate running for office. The irony was that it had been John McCain who encouraged Obama to take this "Commander-in-Chief"-style tour. And it was President Bush – still regarded by most Europeans as a pariah – who Barack Obama had to thank for the record-breaking crowds he attracted abroad.

Since the start of the summer, John McCain had chided Barack Obama for attempting to dictate war policy without having set foot in Iraq in 900 days. That gibe provided rhythm for the Republican theme song in which the Illinois senator was said to be a rookie lacking depth or practical experience in the serious business of managing wars. Barack Obama had never served in the US military and, up against a revered war hero, he was easily cast as a foreign policy naïf. Opinion polls consistently proved that, of the two men, Americans placed greater trust in John McCain to handle a national security crisis.

In late July 2008, however, Barack Obama arrived in Afghanistan as part of a plan to beef up his foreign policy experience. He toured the US military base in Jalalabad and played basketball with some troops billeted there before being flown to Iraq. Other soldiers who stood in 110 degree heat to greet Obama reported back to loved ones that he passed through quickly and did not talk to them. As part of an official Congressional delegation, or "CODEL", Obama had made the trip with Democratic Senator Jack Reed and Republican Senator Chuck Hagel. But locked in a neck-and-neck race for the White House, Senator Obama dominated the July overseas visit.

Pictures relayed back by the US military from the two war zones showed a relaxed Obama conversing with well-known generals and occasionally disagreeing with the top brass. Before travelling, Barack Obama had penned a piece in the *New York Times* confirming his plan to begin troop withdrawal from Iraq during his first sixteen months in office. Additionally, he would redirect some forces to Afghanistan, where Obama felt a more ominous threat to American national security was emerging. In 2008, the US still had 140,000 men and women positioned in various provinces throughout Iraq, some on their second and third tours of duty. US casualties in Iraq had decreased owing to improved security, but in Afghanistan – where the Taliban are backed by foreign fighters – American and NATO casualties were climbing.

"Wrong!" was how John McCain responded to Obama's plan. By shifting troops from one country to the other, McCain charged that Obama was willing to "lose the war in Iraq in order to win one in Afghanistan". But no sooner had McCain delivered his verdict than Iraqi Prime Minister Nouri al-Maliki said he liked Obama's timetable. "Iraqi PM backs Obama troop exit plan" was the title of an email the White House sent to journalists. We wondered if President Bush had indeed departed the Oval Office six months early. Normally his staff hid such reports, played them down, or spun them into oblivion. Now they were emailing them directly to the press!

As it played out, the email had been meant for White House eyes only. But President Bush, too, was moving closer to the concept of an early withdrawal. Just days earlier, without any publicity, Bush and al-Maliki had agreed to set a "general time horizon" for removing troops from Iraqi towns and villages by 2009 and from the provinces by 2011. In the few days surrounding Obama's Iraq visit, the war debate had shifted further and faster than ever before. The idea that America might have a vastly reduced presence in Iraq began to seem real.

It is said that you should be careful what you wish for. As Barack Obama continued the overseas tour that John McCain had goaded him into, the Republican senator was fit to be tied. America's news channels were flooded with images of Obama being ferried by helicopter across mountainous terrain and meeting face-to-face with Iraqi and Afghan leaders. Now in danger of being the lone voice arguing that the US stay in Iraq indefinitely, Senator McCain hightailed it up to Kennebunkport, Maine to confer with George Bush senior. Alas, the only cool toy up at the former president's seaside compound was a golf cart, and evening news images of the Vietnam War hero McCain riding around with the elder Bush had "old guard" written all over it. Seeing his own foreign policy credentials tarnished at the expense of Obama's newly found success would certainly mean a rough ride towards the eighteenth hole in November.

Next stop for Barack Obama was Jerusalem, where his visit went largely unnoticed by the locals. Many Israelis believed Obama to be of Muslim origin and unduly sympathetic to the Palestinian cause. It was an indication that a President Obama might not be starting off with any more leverage than those who had grappled with the Israeli-Palestinian issue before and failed. "The viability of the two-state solution is not going to remain in place indefinitely," said John Bruton, EU Ambassador to Washington, commenting on the speed at which the next president would have to work to make progress. The huge increase in Israeli settlement activity beyond its own protection wall, Bruton believed, meant that soon there would not be enough land left for a Palestinian state. Neither candidate, he felt, had talked enough about the two-state solution. "Public opinion here in the US isn't prepared for the sort of compromises that may be necessary," Bruton said.

But despite the plethora of problems that lay ahead – in Iran, Syria, Lebanon or almost wherever you cared to look on the world map – Barack Obama was having one hell of a week abroad. On 24 July, the Democratic nominee arrived in Europe to address the largest audience of his career.

"People of Berlin, people of the world," Obama began before a crowd of 200,000 Germans basking in the evening sun. Many had been lured to Berlin's Tiergarten by a popular local rock band, but they had also come to give Barack Obama what could be considered to be the "German vote". While Obama claimed to be speaking as "an American citizen" and not as a presidential candidate, it was difficult to ignore the fact that Berliners saw him as America's next leader. They were not alone. A twenty-two-nation survey by the Program on International Policy Attitudes, conducted in the autumn of 2008, showed that if the rest of the world had a vote in the US election Barack Obama was their overwhelming choice.

In Berlin, where the wall between east and west had long ago collapsed, Obama identified new barriers in need of demolition. "The walls between old allies on either side of the Atlantic cannot stand. The walls between the countries with the most and those with the least cannot stand. The walls between races and tribes, natives and immigrants, Christian and Muslim and Jew cannot stand," Obama said.

Harkening back to the first unilateral decision taken by the Bush Administration in early 2001 to pull out of the Kyoto agreement, Senator Obama sent a signal to Europe that it would soon witness an attitudinal sea change on the climate issue. "Nations including my own will act with the same seriousness of purpose as has your nation, and reduce carbon we send into our atmosphere." Deploying his real power, which is to inspire an audience with words, Obama spoke of ending genocide and torture and of bringing hope to those left behind in a globalised world.

"More better than Bush," was the summation of one Berlin resident interviewed on RTÉ after Obama's speech. Despite the Berliner's grammatical mix-up, the sentiment was clear. A President Obama would mean a new beginning for Europe and America. European leaders, John Bruton believed, had already moved beyond their own citizens to re-establish "good relationships" with Washington during George W. Bush's second term. "But that hasn't influenced European public opinion very much," he said. By late 2008, however, it was clear that Obamamania in Europe held out the hope of redemption for America – the prospect of ordinary Europeans forgiving Uncle Sam for the perceived foreign policy mistakes of the past decade.

That feeling of being unloved abroad has slowly eaten into the American psyche. Such negativity towards the United States, I found, had a deeper and longer-lasting effect on some Americans than the terrorist attacks of September 2001. "It's embarrassing" or "I'm ashamed" people of all ages and races told me – mourning how far their country's star has fallen since the opening of the offshore US military prison at Guantanamo Bay and the invasion of Iraq. "I readily acknowledge that we caused some rifts between the nations we definitely want to have the warmest possible relationships with," said Michael Patrick McHugh, a Republican congressman who has Donegal roots. He did not believe, however, that the Iraq war was a political deception. "It was a massive, and by that I mean a global, failure of intelligence. It wasn't just the Bush administration."

As Barack Obama soaked up the German sun, John McCain could have stood on his head and danced naked and no one would have noticed. So McCain's team organised a counter event at a German restaurant in Columbus, Ohio, whose logo is "Make the Best of the Wurst". Asked why he had not visited Germany himself, McCain stated that he would wait until *after* he was elected president to make his own trip to Europe. It was a masterful answer, because at that moment Barack Obama – the presumptive Democratic nominee – became known to his opponents and critics as the "presumptuous nominee".

"It's disgusting!" screamed an Annapolis woman I caught running up West Street on her lunch break the day after Obama's Berlin speech. "He's a candidate, not the president. To represent himself as the voice of America at this point in time is really offensive!" she barked into my microphone, storming off before I could get out a follow-up question.

"It's a peace thing really to me. He's reaching out," said Lenny Kane, an African-American who intended to cast his vote for Obama on election day. "He has great motive," said Emily Kozel, who believed Obama did not need to be president in order to speak positively to Europeans about America. "He said he wanted to break down the barrier between blacks and whites in America. I thought that was great," Kozel concluded.

A group of young people returning to their Annapolis office were more alarmed, however, that Europeans might be trying to tell Americans what to do – as the UN had attempted to do in the run-up to the Iraq war. "They are not the ones that are going to vote for him. We are!" a young woman declared. "They have no votes. He should be over here taking care of us," her friend added, before reminding me that Europeans loved America when it came to exchanging their euro for dollars to do Christmas shopping.

Senator Obama's troubles were compounded by news that he had cancelled a planned visit to injured US soldiers at Germany's Ramstein Air Base. Reports suggested that the Army would not allow a political event to be held with campaign aides present, and that as a result Obama's team had pulled out. Within hours, Republicans had a publicity coup on their hands and were running a television advertisement claiming that Barack Obama had snubbed America's injured soldiers in favour of a gym work-out.

At the end of a week in which he had triumphed in the Tiergarten and attracted worldwide exposure, Obama was taking a beating in the polls at home. The small lead he had held over John McCain since the early summer evaporated, and the race for the White House was closer than ever. If Barack Obama was not already on the back foot as he returned to American soil, the next wave of assaults from the newly re-tooled Republican attack machine was designed to floor him.

"HE'S THE BIGGEST CELEBRITY IN the world" was how one of the most memorable television ads of the 2008 presidential season began. A baritone voice spoke over footage of Barack Obama addressing the cheering Berlin crowd. Then, into the scene an editor inserted images of blonde pop star Britney Spears and socialite Paris Hilton. "But is he ready to lead?" the voice asked. The intended message was that Barack Obama was more Hollywood than Washington – more bling than king.

Even Paris Hilton, the heiress and ubiquitous goodtime girl, was moved to react with a television spot of her own. "They put me in their ad, so I guess I'm running for president," Hilton announced, clad in a leopard print bikini, as she gamely volunteered solutions to America's problems. With their thirty-second advertisement, the Republican team had turned the Berlin speech into an example of what they saw as Obama's "empty celebrity".

"There will always be an audience for that message," an Obama campaign insider mused at the time. "But I think a lot of people are happy that an American politician can go abroad and create excitement. More than anything, what motivated people to join us was the feeling of lost leadership – a feeling that the country had lost its way as an international leader and that Obama offered a way back towards that," the insider noted.

When Russian tanks rolled into Georgia in early August 2008, Barack Obama was caught looking a bit like a Hollywood celebrity as he vacationed with his family in Hawaii. As Russia flexed its muscles, images of the young Illinois senator body-surfing in the waves did little to reassure Americans of his leadership abilities. Meanwhile, John McCain was talking tough. "We are all Georgians now," McCain exclaimed, except that some Americans assumed he was referring to their beloved "Peach State" below Tennessee and South Carolina!

Georgia's crisis echoed the Iraq conflict in that it involved a lethal mix of democracy and oil – specifically an oil pipeline coming out of Russia and running through Georgia. Fear of Russia controlling the flow of oil had sent Republican congressman Steve King of Iowa to Tbilisi at the height of the crisis to protest, in solidarity with Georgians. "Imagine Vladimir Putin standing there with a big valve, and he can turn the oil on to go east or west," King explained. Should Putin form an alliance with Iran, 50 per cent of the world's cheap oil could flow to China instead of to western countries. "That's the game that's going on," King told me, adding that he thought Barack Obama had no clue how to handle it. Republicans, King said, would like to bring Georgia into NATO and encourage the construction of a separate pipeline to guarantee the westward flow of oil.

Obama was not short of foreign policy advisers telling him what was going on; he had 300 of them. But Senator Obama still needed to convince Americans that he could handle a major crisis. Voters longed for a leader who could improve America's image abroad, but they also wanted someone who would not be pushed around. Barack Obama understood that he needed a running mate with extensive foreign policy experience. Joe Biden's name shot to the top of the list.

Politics is a strange game. One day you are down, the next day you are back up. Joe Biden, a long-time senator from Delaware, had crashed in the first of the Democratic primary races – winning less than one per cent of the vote in the Iowa caucus. The 2008 race was Biden's second run for the presidency, having tried two decades earlier with no luck. Journalists knew him as a bit of a blowhard. He liked to take credit, was prone to verbal gaffes and craved the media spotlight. Senator Biden even entertained lowly foreign reporters, but we knew nothing about his hardscrabble beginnings or his tragic life story.

Joe Biden was born to an Irish-American working-class family in the town of Scranton in northeastern Pennsylvania. In the 1940s, Scranton was in the doldrums and, to find work, the family had moved south to Delaware. Joe Biden's father sold cars, and eventually the Bidens joined the middle class. Joe married, had three children, entered local politics, and by age thirty was elected to the US Senate. But within weeks of his victory in 1972, Biden's wife and baby daughter were killed in a car crash while out holiday shopping. Two young sons, also in the car, were badly injured. Joe Biden was sworn into the US Senate at the hospital bedside of one of his boys. One thing that attracted Barack Obama to Joe Biden was that he had successfully balanced his home life and politics. Senator Biden had never moved to Washington DC. Rather, every night for thirty-six years he took the train back to Wilmington, Delaware to be with his family. In 1977, Joe Biden married English teacher Jill Jacobs. The story goes that he had to propose five times before she agreed be his wife, because Jill Jacobs knew she would be buying into a busy political future. "It was Joe, the boys and the state of Delaware," she has said of her decision to become Jill Biden.

In June 2008, the Obama campaign informed Joe Biden that they were "vetting" him for the position of vice-president. That meant asking for personal records to ensure there were no embarrassing skeletons in Biden's closet that could damage the ticket. Senator Biden didn't appear excited and let it be publicly known that he might decline any offer to be Obama's number two. By mid-August, however, Obama was in need of Biden's experience as Chairman of the US Senate Committee on Foreign Relations. Biden was also twenty years older than Obama, an age difference that would lend gravitas to the ticket. Topping it all off, Senator Biden came from blue-collar stock back in Scranton, Pennsylvania – the type of people Obama wanted to impress before November.

At a hotel in St Paul, Minnesota, well away from the media, a top secret meeting took place between Obama and Biden. For three hours they talked about the kind of working relationship that would be necessary. Obama was straight with Biden. "Will this job be too small for you?" he asked. Biden replied that as long as he could really be a confidant in Obama's White House, the two could work together. Joe Biden would want a weekly lunch with the president, just as Al Gore had with Bill Clinton. He would also want to be present at key meetings and have an input into decision-making.

Senator Joe Biden returned to Delaware where he found the press camped out at the gates of his house. For the next several days he drove in and out past the bank of cameras – even offering coffee and doughnuts to the journalists – but Biden said nothing. Barack Obama would announce his choice for vice-president in his own way and in his own time.

"WELCOME TO SADDLEBACK!" WITH THOSE words the first television debate of the autumn 2008 season got underway. It was not supposed to rank as a real presidential debate, just a chat in a California church. But with John McCain and Barack Obama tied in the polls, it was a chance to see what separated them. Saddleback is a mega-church run by evangelical pastor Rick Warren, an author whose book *The Purpose Driven Life* is one of the best-selling non-fiction books of all time.

Warren, a jovial-looking man in his fifties, likes everything big. He is physically big, his church is big, its membership is big, and on 16 August 2008 his television audience for the first showdown between the presidential candidates was several million. Though not on the formal political calendar, the event was essentially a political debate held in a church and moderated by a pastor. Welcome to America. In a country founded on Judeo-Christian values, such a show barely raised an eyebrow.

Demonstrating that they both knew on which side their evangelical bread was buttered, Barack Obama told the audience that "Jesus Christ died for my sins, and I am redeemed through Him". John McCain announced that he was "saved and forgiven". That was where the similarity ended.

"At what stage does a baby get human rights?" Pastor Rick asked Obama. After muttering about theological considerations, Obama concluded that the answer was "above my pay grade". In the green room his handlers must have sunk low into their seats. When John McCain's turn came to respond to the same query, he pulled the face of a pub quiz contestant who had rehearsed his answer just hours earlier. "At the moment of conception!" McCain blurted to wild audience applause.

Barack Obama had come to a difficult venue in the hope of winning over moderate evangelicals. In recent years religious voters have added climate change, genocide in Darfur and Third World debt to their list of traditional concerns. But those broader issues were barely addressed. Instead, Pastor Rick stuck to themes associated with the culture wars and with the George W. Bush era.

"Does evil exist? And if it does, do we confront it, negotiate with it, ignore it or defeat it?" Rick Warren asked John McCain. "Defeat it!" Senator McCain answered before the questioner had finished. "And if I have to follow him to the gates of hell, I will bring Osama Bin Laden to justice!" he bellowed, the crowd cheering him on. Barack Obama's more cerebral answer about finding evil on America's own streets, in Guantanamo Bay or Abu Ghraib was not what this evangelical audience was hoping for. "He may as well be back in Berlin making speeches to the Berliners," intoned right-wing talk radio king Rush Limbaugh, referring to Obama's performance. John McCain was deemed to be the night's winner.

The chat in the church confirmed how deeply split America remained on the same old issues. To me, it felt like 2000 or 2004 all over again. I questioned how Barack Obama had ever believed that he could join Red America with Blue America to become the President of the United States of America.

I was beginning to wonder too if either of these two candidates had the patriotic grace needed to truly transform this collection of fifty states. John McCain and Barack Obama were the smartest of men, but they still appealed to opposing factions who insisted on sniping at each other across a deep cultural and ideological divide. I recalled how in the days after 11 September 2001, America had been united in its grief, but as the sadness receded, so did the harmony. Somehow a precious opportunity had been lost, and old conflicts returned to pit Republicans against Democrats and liberals against conservatives. The state-by-state electoral system, it seemed, was set up to reinforce these divisions. Another close presidential election was not what America needed.

TO BROADEN HIS ELECTORAL APPEAL, John McCain toyed with the notion of picking Tom Ridge as his vice-presidential running mate. Ridge, from Pennsylvania, was a former head of the Department of Homeland Security, but he was pro-choice, which caused heartburn for conservatives. Joe Lieberman, an independent Democrat and close friend, appealed to McCain's "Maverick" side, but Lieberman was also for abortion rights. Signals were quickly sent that, if either man was on the ticket, the "base" might skip the 2008 election and not vote. One such message posted on the website of *The Nation*, a left-wing magazine, by a writer called "pontificus" summed up how everyone was retreating into their comfy old corners. "Of course McCain isn't going to pick a pro-choicer. It'd be political suicide. He has to 'pay off' his base by nominating someone who thinks life begins when you have sex, and that we should mandate the Lord's Prayer at all school lunches. He can't 'Go Maverick', or the hard right will stay at home on November 4th and say, 'Let the Commie, Muslim, Black guy win.... We'll get a real conservative in 2012'."

With unsolicited advice like that, John McCain was under pressure to pick a pro-life vice-presidential candidate who would appeal to America's conservative base. He had run across someone at a national gathering of state governors a few months earlier who might fit the bill. He would have to look her up.

On the Saturday morning before the Denver Democratic convention, Barack Obama sent word about his vice-presidential choice via text message at 3 a.m. saying, "I have some important news that I want to make official. I've chosen Joe Biden to be my running mate." The irony of Obama's middle of the night text message was not lost on anyone. It was a reminder of the famous 3 a.m. phone call advert which Hillary Clinton had used against him back at the height of the primary season. Clinton had intended to show that Obama was not equipped to deal with a foreign policy crisis at three in the morning. Now Barack Obama was sending his own clear message that – with Senator Joe Biden by his side – he would be ready at *any* time of the day or night.

11

Unity at Last

*"Everything I learned in my eight years as president,
and in the work I have done since in America and across
the globe, has convinced me that Barack Obama is the
man for this job."* – BILL CLINTON

THE WOMAN ON THE F TRAIN from downtown Denver to the
suburb of Lincoln was in a state of disarray. Her mascara
had run, giving her raccoon eyes, her hair was in need of
brushing, and her "Hillary for President" t-shirt was a dead
give-away that she was one of the bitter-enders trying to turn
Barack Obama's nominating convention into a requiem for the
Clinton candidacy.

"I still believe she'll be nominated. I just have this feeling, I
really do," she blurted, causing other passengers to turn
around and stare. "I'm going to vote for John McCain if Hillary
is not nominated," she declared.

It was Monday night, the end of day one of the Democratic
convention, and the air around Denver's Pepsi Center was
thick with rumours of plots to disrupt the process for selecting
Barack Obama as the Democratic Party's presidential nominee.

There would be loud protests and walkouts. The achievements of the first woman of American politics had been discounted. Hillary's people would raise hell, and we had better be ready for fireworks. In truth, we had been ready for months. The promise of a rancorous floor fight had lured 50,000 blood-thirsty onlookers to Colorado. Conspiracy theories abounded, yet nobody really expected a stunning turn of events that would see Hillary run off with the crown – except maybe the woman sitting opposite me.

"What good would all that do?" I asked, referring to her plan to abandon her party if Hillary Clinton did not pull off an upset. "I'm from Florida," she responded. "We've been badly treated by the Democrats there. We're shattered into a thousand pieces."

It had been months since the Democratic National Committee had penalised Clinton-leaning Florida and Michigan for holding their primaries too early. Half of those two states' delegates were now prohibited from voting at the nominating convention, but there had been plenty of time to face the facts and move on. Judging by her appearance, however, this Hillary holdout was still in full combat mode. She fished a map from her pocket and showed me the route Clinton supporters intended to march along the following morning to highlight the perceived injustice to the sisterhood. Then the doors of the F train opened, and the woman disappeared into the night. I never asked her name, but by the end of the week she would be known as one of the PUMAs – the "Party Unity My Ass" crowd.

There were two Democratic conventions in Denver that August. The first was the Clinton convention, a catharsis for those delegates and supporters who had not yet given up their dream of seeing Hillary Clinton become America's first woman president. Until they could vent their disappointment in public, they would not be backing Barack Obama. With the aid of a hyperventilating press more interested in splits than love-ins, the Clinton theatrics ran for the first three days of convention week. Barack Obama had only the final evening to sell himself to the American public.

For months in advance, Colorado's capital city of Denver had been booked solid by the Democratic Party and enthusiasts accustomed to the machinations of these huge events. A friend and I had pre-booked a room, which was advertised as "south of the city". Though it turned out to be considerably farther south than we had bargained for, we felt lucky to have a place to sleep. Every politico and pundit on the planet had schemed and plotted to be in Denver.

Conventions allow a party's delegates to meet and nominate their candidate for president and vice-president. But in 2008, delegates accounted for just one in ten of those who turned up in Denver. For every delegate, there were three journalists, plus thousands of political consultants, strategists and pollsters. So long as you looked the part and had a contacts book large enough to keep you on the phone all day, you could blend in there. Business and labour interests were well represented, as were company executives who donated considerable sums to the Democratic Party and felt entitled to network and lobby late into the night. At the fancier downtown hotels were Washington politicians and their families, the occasional Hollywood celebrity, as well as ambassadors from around the world.

The biggest political trade show on the planet was not without Irish representation. By day two, I ran into a group of politicians being hosted by the National Democratic Institute or NDI – the Washington non-profit organisation chaired by former Secretary of State Madeleine Albright. Although they paid their own way and sat through daily forums on how to spread good government around the globe, Fianna Fáil's Noel Dempsey and Mary Hanafin, Labour Party leader Eamon Gilmore and former leader Ruairi Quinn were among 600 international politicians who obtained ringside seats to the unfolding events. Others present included Fine Gael leader Enda Kenny, former Justice Minister Nora Owen and Deputies Olwyn Enright and Joe McHugh.

Gaining entry to Denver's Pepsi Center was like making a mini-pilgrimage to Mecca. Two miles from the stadium, public transport ended and foot traffic or rickshaw taxis took over. The building itself was protected by a triple layer of security. On more than one occasion, I left friends at the outer perimeter, as they waited to secure entry passes that were swapped and traded like an addict acquiring a daily fix of narcotics. "Out dealing since 6 a.m.!" read a text message from Sighle Doherty, when I inquired if she could help us find extra seats for key speeches. Sighle, then associated with the NDI, spent much of the convention week using both her own and husband Ivan Doherty's extensive contacts to obtain top tickets from Democratic National Committee members.

Inside the first gate surrounding the Pepsi Center, I hit a wall of several thousand people waiting to clear airport-like security checks. In the August heat and humidity, it was difficult to fathom why so many women came in stiletto heels, designer pant suits and lacquered heads – suited more for a wedding than a good old-fashioned political dust-up. The only thing missing were printed invitations to the on-again off-again marriage of convenience between the Clintons and Obamas. For all this glitz, the security line was a tense place where people stared anxiously at their watches and anyone caught jumping the queue ran the risk of being escorted to the rear by the nearest policeman.

Your first peek inside a large convention hall is breathtaking. Passing through the portals into the arena is like entering the Roman Coliseum. All the way around, sections are brimming with chattering guests, and countless divisions sweep naturally down to the centre stage where all the action will occur. In America, no matter what the year or the party, it's always a sea of red, white and blue. And as portable technology has caught on, political arenas are now further illuminated by the screens of laptops, Blackberries and camera phones.

Jerry Kellman, who hired Barack Obama as a community organiser, was addressing Democrats when I arrived. I had talked to Jerry about Obama's work in Chicago during the 1980s and was eager to hear his take on the candidate's fitness for the presidency, but I was only one of a small number listening. The incessant banter among delegates and the coming and going of the media down on the convention floor all but drowned out Kellman. Up in the stands, Democrats who had spent hours getting into the event were already preoccupied with emailing and texting.

Recovering from surgery to treat his brain cancer, someone arrived who *could* silence the crowd. Though he did not receive the twenty-two minute standing ovation given to his brother Bobby at the 1964 Atlantic City convention following JFK's assassination, Senator Edward Kennedy's surprise appearance lent a touch of old Kennedy magic to the proceedings and a welcome diversion from the Clinton-Obama disunity problem.

Like his brothers before him, the Massachusetts senator had the gift of elevating politics to the order of religion. "There is a new wave of change," he declared. "And if we set our compass true, we will reach our destination." The ailing senator contended that by electing Barack Obama as president, Americans could choose "renewal for our nation".

"Ted Kennedy, we'd die for him," a woman near to me sobbed, as the senator was joined on stage by his extended family. For a few moments, distant flashes of Camelot lit up the Denver night as the current generation embraced the last of the fabled brothers. "The dream lives on!" Ted Kennedy proclaimed, entrusting the hopes of former Democratic giants to the care of the young bloods.

The woman who came on stage next to explain how her husband would handle these hopes had changed. Gone was the feisty, straight-talking Michelle Obama who earlier in the campaign was apt to let loose on a range of topics, including her husband's untidy habits and smelly socks! In her place was a more subdued speaker. Her lines learned and cadences practiced, Mrs Obama told fluffy family stories designed to fight the growing whispers from the American right that the Obamas of Chicago's Hyde Park were too "elitist" or "different" to occupy the White House.

"Barack and I were raised with so many of the same values," Michelle Obama said, explaining that you "work hard for what you want in life, that your word is your bond and you do what you say you're going to do". Barack Obama's working-class grandparents, she told the assembled Democrats, had sacrificed much to fund his education. And in her own family, Michelle's father had developed multiple sclerosis in his thirties but continued to work at a Chicago water sanitation plant, a job he never liked, until his death. "He never stopped smiling and laughing, even while struggling to button his shirt, even while needing two canes to get himself across the room to give my mom a kiss," she told the hushed audience, nailing her point that the Obamas' personal stories were far from elitist.

Barack Obama's "patriotism problem" – though manufactured by his critics – was not insignificant. On numerous occasions I met people who believed that Obama had refused to recite the Pledge of Allegiance, or that he had taken his oath of office in the US Senate on the Koran. Michelle's earlier comment, "I am proud of my country for the first time in my adult life", provided fodder to those who felt the Obamas did not love America. The Obamas' famous "fist bump" was incorrectly interpreted as a terrorist salute, and a *New Yorker* cartoon of the couple in black activist and Muslim garb designed to poke fun had just made the situation worse. "I love this country!" Michelle Obama declared in Denver, attempting to bat away the controversies. But her main role that night was to speak warmly as the mother of two young daughters and proud wife of the man she hoped would be president.

Yet as the new First Lady, Mrs Obama would be a long leap from the list of Anglo-America women who had occupied the East Wing before her. A certain level of imagination was required to see Michelle Obama in the role played by Jackie Kennedy, Nancy Reagan, Barbara and Laura Bush, or even the trail-blazing Hillary Clinton. Despite the softer persona she displayed at the Democratic convention, her supporters were in little doubt that – once Michelle Obama made it to the White House – the more sassy, Harvard-educated lawyer would re-emerge. Obama's combination of style, smarts and common sense would allow her to fashion an entirely new model for First Lady.

"I don't think she's going to be counting the china in the dining room or planning the menus," said Maureen Fiedler, a radio broadcaster from Maryland. "I would expect her to have real input into the public policy of the country, perhaps a role not unlike what Hillary Clinton performed in Bill Clinton's administration."

Until recently, political wives at conventions were seen and not heard. Their task was to look glamorous, as in Jackie Kennedy's case, or suitably stern, like Harry Truman's wife Bess, who the thirty-third US president referred to as "The Boss". Nancy Reagan did not address the Republican convention until her husband was seeking re-election in 1984, and though Laura Bush developed a confident style of her own, she entered the White House with an aversion to public speaking. In contrast, Michelle Obama owned the first night at the 2008 Democratic convention, and it was just as well. For the next two days, it became the "Bill and Hillary Show".

EVEN AS SHE BOWED OUT OF THE PRIMARY race, Hillary Clinton refused to say if this was the end of the story. By June 2008, Clinton had endorsed Obama, but since both candidates had won a high number of delegates, there was still the question of what would happen in Denver. As a result, two Democratic camps arrived at the Pepsi Center – a Clinton camp and an Obama camp – neither knowing what the other wanted to do about the formal nominating process.

Clinton's loyal supporters had asked for Hillary's name to be put into nomination to allow her delegates to vote their preference. This would provide public recognition of Clinton's remarkable achievement and offer her delegates a way to move forward with Obama. But for almost half the delegates to declare support for Hillary Clinton at Barack Obama's nominating convention would make Obama look weak. A suggestion that the roll calls be held at delegate breakfasts, away from the glare of the convention floor, did not fly. Caught between the demands of her supporters and the need for unity, Hillary Clinton eventually released her 1,639 pledged delegates and her hundreds of superdelegates to vote for Obama if they so wished.

"I'm still voting for Hillary," said a Minnesota delegate who was among the first to get wind of the compromise eventually worked out between the Clinton and Obama campaigns. "On the roll call, we will vote for Hillary. Halfway through, she will suspend the rules and declare Obama the nominee," he said.

From where Nora Owen saw the drama unfold, former President Bill Clinton appeared to have lukewarm feelings towards Barack Obama. Bill Clinton had addressed Owen and the guests of the National Democratic Institute and initially left her cold. "He never mentioned Obama by name at all. In fact, the only reference he made was more or less a negative one," said Owen. "He said there are candidates who only promise what they think they can deliver, and there are others who promise everything and can never deliver. It was a real direct hit, I felt, at Obama. And that's the way it was taken by people listening." A day later Bill Clinton would make a convincing argument for Obama's candidacy, but no matter how Clinton tried, his innermost feelings would be questioned until the campaign's final week. On the other hand, during the historic roll call vote in Denver, Hillary Clinton gamely made the switch from competitor to supporter.

"Mississippi, how do you cast your vote?" asked the convention secretary as the roll call hit its midpoint. From the start, it was clear that most of Hillary Clinton's delegates had switched their support to Barack Obama. "Mississippi, the home of the late Fannie Lou Hamer, casts eight votes for Hillary Clinton and thirty-three votes for the next president of the United States, Barack Obama," the Mississippi representative replied, slipping in the mention of the state's famed civil rights leader. New Hampshire, where Hillary Clinton had made her first big comeback in January, cast its entire vote for Barack Obama and New Jersey did the same. When called upon to deliver its vote, Senator Obama's adopted home state of Illinois yielded to Clinton's adopted state of New York.

"New York, you have two hundred and eighty-two votes. How do you cast them?" the secretary asked. With members of her delegation huddled around her, Hillary Clinton cast away any remaining possibility of her long held 2008 presidential dream. In a strong and purposeful voice she said, "In the spirit of unity, with the goal of victory, with faith in our party and our country, let's declare together in one voice – right here, right now – that Barack Obama is our candidate and he will be our president."

As Clinton sealed Obama's nomination, tears flowed in the arena – not for one woman's lost dream, but for the newly born hopes of an entire race that had waited so long to see a black man reach such heights in America. "Is there a second?" asked the secretary. "Yes!" roared the crowd. "All those in favour, please say 'Aye'." "Aye!" 10,000 voices thundered, and it was done.

"I was so proud to be an American," said Mike Coleman, an African-American state delegate and mayor of Columbus,

Ohio. By the time I caught up with him, Coleman had dried his eyes, but he was certain that he had just taken part in the most incredible experience of his life – nominating the first black man for president of the United States. "The American dream was not always the African-American reality," Coleman said, his eyes beginning to well again. "Now, for the first time, I think people believe that dream can come true."

Evelyn Leonard from Virginia had reached her eightieth birthday and had to pinch herself. "From what I've seen growing up, I would never believe that this would ever happen," she said, though she suspected it would take more than a nomination to erase the scourge of racism. "Some people will never vote for Barack Obama – no matter how smart he is, no matter how qualified, no matter how much he could change the world for the better. They won't vote for him because of the color of his skin," Leonard said. As they led her away, Evelyn's two daughters nodded in agreement. "It used to be they wouldn't vote for an Irish Catholic!" daughter Marguerite Rogers shouted back to me.

For Majid al-Bahadli, a Democratic delegate from the northwest state of Washington, Obama's nomination pointed to a new start of a different kind. "My Iraqi family can't wait until Senator Obama becomes president and liberates their homeland," he said, explaining that he himself had taken part in the popular uprising against Saddam Hussein after the first Gulf War in 1991. George Bush senior asked Iraqis to rise up, but Majid was taken prisoner in Iraq and jailed for five years before escaping to America as a refugee. "We have no reason to stay in Iraq," he said, claiming that it was time for his American brothers to "stop hurting" his Iraqi brothers.

I ARRIVED LATE THAT NIGHT for Bill Clinton's endorsement of Barack Obama. The seated part of the arena was already full, and even overflow spots around the television screens outside the main hall contained hundreds of people jammed together. As I strained to see Bill Clinton over the shoulders of those in front of me, it was obvious that the agitated old codger who had blundered his way along the primary election trail had been replaced by the former president at his very best. Even if he believed only half of what he said, Bill Clinton made it sound as though Barack Obama was America's last best hope.

"Clearly the job of the next president is to restore the American dream and to restore American leadership in the world. Everything I learned in my eight years as president, and in the work I have done since in America and across the globe, has convinced me that Barack Obama is the man for this job," Bill Clinton said.

Since leaving office in January 2001, Clinton had made almost $50 million from speaking engagements – so he knew how to spin a line. To hear him more clearly, I slipped into the ladies bathroom where his speech was being piped through the ceiling speakers. There I had a seat and the perfect place to write. "My candidate didn't win," the former president acknowledged, but in his praise of the victor he exceeded all expectations. By the time he concluded, Bill Clinton had left the Republicans in tatters and passed the Democratic chalice to Obama. It was time to move on.

Later that evening, when Joe Biden accepted his nomination as vice-president, I was thinking about what the black woman and her daughter Marguerite had said. Nearly half a century ago, Catholics had overcome similar stereotypes to those Barack Obama was conquering in 2008. The election of

John F. Kennedy in 1960 had been enabling, so much so that nobody batted an eyelid when Joe Biden – a former altar boy and the son of Catherine Finnegan – now aspired to the office of vice-president.

"When the big boys would knock me down, she'd tell me to get back out there and bloody their noses!" Joe Biden told Democrats, as cameras moved to show the snowy-haired Mrs Biden in the VIP section. But for all the laughter in the arena, I could not envision Barack Obama telling such a story about a member of his own family. A black man entering a white man's game at the highest level had to refrain from telling tales of street fights or bloody noses. After fifty years at the top, the Irish could say what they pleased, but the African-American still had to mind his Ps & Qs.

ON THE AFTERNOON OF BARACK OBAMA'S acceptance speech before a record-breaking 84,000 people, Democratic strategist Anne Sullivan breezed into the Capital Grille in downtown Denver. There's a restaurant of the same name in Washington DC, but on 28 August it seemed as if the whole of the nation's capital had migrated to Denver for lunch. Congressmen and senators huddled in corners, and sharply dressed political types barked demands into cell phones as television networks compared the impending event to Dr Martin Luther King's "I have a dream speech" delivered exactly forty-five years earlier.

"I have one more pass," Anne Sullivan announced to our table, as she ran though her contacts list to see if she could muster another. Joining me at the restaurant were Sara Aiken from Annapolis and Norman Houston, who runs the Northern Ireland Bureau in Washington. Both friends had now scored good seats to hear Barack Obama speak at Invesco Field, and though I had media access I was aching to experience the reaction of the crowd rather than be stuck with 15,000 journalists.

"Call me. I might have something soon!" Anne shouted back, as she rushed away to her next appointment.

"Happy Birthday!" Sara said, sliding her laminated pass across the table and offering to take my flimsy media credential. Moments later, news arrived that leftover passes were being distributed halfway across the city. With Denver under tight security lockdown for Obama's arrival, Sara – the fittest of the bunch – took off on foot to join yet another scrum for tickets. For all her marvellous effort, we ended sitting next to each other at Invesco Field, the Denver Bronco's football stadium.

Whatever it is about the sound of so many people cheering and shouting, the silence of vast crowds is even more impressive. As the evening sun disappeared below the horizon, the air became still in the arena. The reason for the hush was the baby picture that had appeared on big screens all around us.

"Who calls their kid Barack Obama?" asked Michelle Obama, setting off a torrent of laughter as a film showed Michelle recalling the first time she heard her husband's name. There were wedding pictures and the now familiar shots of Barack Obama working on Chicago's South Side, as well as Obama teaching class at the University of Chicago Law School. As if to illustrate the warp speed of his political ascent, we next saw Senator Obama on the steps of Capitol Hill in Washington, but nothing was quite as arresting as the image that followed.

Back on stage, the fully lit set looked remarkably like 1600 Pennsylvania Avenue. Right down to the white sash windows, royal blue carpet, American flags and the rounded podium, the scene evoked that part of the White House familiar to most viewers from television dramas such as *The West Wing*.

"Does it remind you of anything?" I asked a fourteen-year-old Denver boy, who had come with his mother to hear Obama. "The Oval Office," he replied, so I knew I wasn't dreaming. Then candidate Obama came through the centre doors, as if he was entering the Oval Office itself. Bringing Obama's acceptance speech to a large outdoor venue, his campaign managers risked tagging him again as a celebrity candidate. But with their reminiscent stage set, Obama's team had executed an even bolder move by providing an early glimpse of "President Obama" in the White House.

Despite the stagecraft, Obama's task was as gargantuan as his audience. His talent as a speaker was not in doubt, but his ability to sway enough independent voters continued to be in question. Though battle-hardened by a long campaign, Obama was still a relatively inexperienced executive, he remained a mystery to many, and he had yet to win over the mostly female PUMAs. Back at his ranch in Arizona, John McCain was also eyeing the "Party Unity My Ass" crowd and was working on a plan to seek their votes in November while unifying his own conservative base.

"I accept your nomination for the Presidency of the United States!" Obama boomed, surveying multitudes with the confidence of a man without a nerve in his body. Watching him for over a year, it became clear that Barack Obama's performance matched the size of the audience. Before a small crowd, he rarely roused himself to his full potential. But when the numbers warranted it, he pulled out all the stops. Before the huge gathering that Denver evening, Barack Obama's tone was more serious, his jaw more fixed, and his gaze more distant – as he set out his arguments for a Democratic presidency:

"Tonight, more Americans are out of work, and more are working harder for less. More of you have lost your homes, and even more are watching your home values plummet. More of you have cars you can't afford to drive, credit card bills you can't afford to pay, and tuition that's beyond your reach. These challenges are not all of government's making. But the failure to respond is a direct result of broken politics in Washington and the failed policies of George W. Bush. America, we are better than these last eight years. We are a better country than this. This country is more decent than one where a woman in Ohio, on the brink of retirement, finds herself one illness away from disaster after a lifetime of hard work. This country is more generous than one where a man in Indiana has to pack up the equipment he's worked on for twenty years and watch it shipped off to China, and then chokes up as he explains how he felt like a failure when he went home to tell his family the news. We are more compassionate than a government that lets veterans sleep on our streets and families slide into poverty; that sits on its hands while a major American city drowns before our eyes. Tonight, I say to the American people, to Democrats and Republicans and Independents across this great land – enough!"

In a speech that lasted forty-five minutes, Senator Obama put the failing economy at the heart of his campaign. Internal polling carried out by his staff over the summer showed it was what most Americas would vote on. Though it was a long way from his initial rationale for running – ending the Iraq War and bringing change to Washington – Obama knew that worries about financial security would be where the 2008 race was won or lost.

With this in mind, Obama attacked the Republican philosophy of giving more to those with the most in the hope that wealth would trickle down. "What it really means is you're on your own," he said. Democrats, Obama claimed, would measure progress by "how many people can find a job that pays the mortgage". He would cut taxes for 95 per cent of Americans, he promised tax breaks to companies who created jobs at home instead of sending work abroad and, as part of his "Apollo Project", to build a green energy economy, Obama would invest $150 billion over ten years.

Looking overseas, Obama vowed to renew "direct diplomacy" to deal with Iran, curb Russian aggression and end the Iraq war. "You don't defeat a terrorist network that operates in eighty countries by occupying Iraq," Obama suggested. "You don't protect Israel and deter Iran just by talking tough in Washington. If John McCain wants to follow George Bush with more tough talk and bad strategy, that is his choice. But it is not the change we need."

A "symphony" was how former presidential adviser David Gergen described Obama's speech. "The best convention speech in history" was the verdict of Republican commentator Pat Buchanan. Ordinary Democrats I spoke to were less effusive but nonetheless enthused. "He's just magic!" said a woman from Maryland, adding that "He's in for the fight of his life, but he's up to it." "Pretty weird!" another man commented, likening the whole scene to a Nuremburg rally and describing Obama's pledge to reduce taxes for working families as "pure bullshit".

"Where are the balloons?" Sara asked as we got ready to leave, noting that political conventions always ended with a release of red, white and blue balloons. Just then, fireworks erupted noisily into the night sky as Barack Obama's family joined him in front of the White House set. It felt and looked like inauguration night, five months early.

Considering that 50,000 political junkies and journalists were making their way home, the Denver airport was an unexpected oasis of calm the following morning. After a week spent marinating in memorable moments, we were truly pickled. A group of us grabbed an early flight, and as we stared blankly at the television by Gate 28B, the next wave of political intrigue hit us. Ten hours had not yet passed since Barack Obama's stadium speech, and John McCain was already presenting his pick for vice-president. "Her name is Sarah Palin," a CNN reporter announced.

"Sarah who?"

"What?"

"Jeez!"

The chorus of expletives from Democrats in line grew louder as the flight was called to board. Passengers were groggy, and many had not had their morning coffee. Was this a joke?

At first glance, it looked as though John McCain had handed Barack Obama the presidency on a platter. But the fun was only beginning.

12

The Lipstick Wars

*"She is going to bring this party up!" "She's perfect ...
She's pro-life, and she's a shooter!"–* SARAH PALIN
SUPPORTERS

"**S**ARAH BARRACUDA" WAS WHAT THEY called her on the high
school basketball team. To Alaskans she was "Caribou
Barbie". But in St Paul, Minnesota, in late August 2008, the
question on everyone's lips as the Republicans took centre
stage was, "Who is Governor Sarah Palin"? Instead of choosing
a predictable Mitt Romney or even a left of field cross-over
candidate like the Democrat Joe Lieberman, John McCain
stunned the political and pundit classes by selecting a forty-
four-year-old mother of five, who two years earlier was the
mayor of Wasilla, Alaska, population 6,700.

Topping that, Sarah Palin is a former beauty queen who
calls her husband the "First Dude" and has sons named Trig
and Track. Though born a Catholic, Palin belongs to a variety
of Pentecostal and Evangelical churches, and at least once has
been cleansed of witchcraft. Whether it is the Alaskan frontier
mentality or the magnetic pull of the North Pole, John

McCain's new lady could not be described as your regular Washington politician.

"She is the antidote to what's wrong with Washington," said South Carolina Senator Lindsey Graham, who I figured might have the inside story. As a close friend and adviser to John McCain throughout the 2008 presidential campaign, Graham knew McCain's innermost thoughts. All Graham would tell me though, on the first night in St Paul, was that the hottest governor from the coldest state was one to watch. "What she has done in Alaska is to shake up a state that was full of corruption," said Senator Graham, predicting that Palin would quickly turn the nation's capital upside down.

The Palin pick had the hallmark of one of John McCain's last minute gambles, but his advisers had her in the mix for a while. Steve Schmidt had been pushing hard for Palin rather than Lieberman, and at the Republican convention a number of key supporters also claimed to have been rooting for her all along. Yet Palin's cross-country dash to meet John McCain for one hour at his Arizona ranch just days before the official announcement looked like an arranged marriage, and dispatching a "Truth Squad" to Alaska to handle nosey journalists made it appear as if the bride had not been fully vetted.

Checked out or not, the gun-toting governor would be worth the risk, according to Minnesota's Republican Senator Norm Coleman. "It sends a message that it won't be business as usual in Washington under John McCain," said Senator Coleman, who later found himself fighting for his own Senate seat, having being challenged by a Democratic comedian. Coleman predicted that voters in his icy-cold state would quickly warm up to the new woman in American politics. "We like moms who can lace up ice skates and ride snowmobiles and who belong to the National Rifle Association," Coleman said, referring to Palin's penchant for posing with all types of sporting and military rifles. Governor Palin had grown up shooting wildlife and was the first candidate in living memory who knew how to "field dress a moose" – a polite term for cleaning and gutting a 1,200 pound animal prior to butchering. "I know how to castrate a calf. Neither of those things has anything at all to do with this election," remarked Democratic Lieutenant Governor Patty Judge, a mother of three, cow farmer and Iowa's first female Secretary of Agriculture, when she learned of Palin's talents.

"I felt insulted as a woman in politics," said former Irish Justice Minister Nora Owen, who saw McCain's pick as troubling. "They were just ticking the boxes," said Owen, who felt Sarah Palin had been chosen purely because the Alaskan governor was a working mother with a son heading off to Iraq. "That kind of tokenism doesn't do women in politics any good," said Owen, who discussed McCain's choice with international female leaders before leaving Denver's Democratic convention. Former Ronald Reagan speechwriter Peggy Noonan was of like mind, describing Sarah Palin's selection as "political bullshit" in an unguarded moment on national television. Noonan's faux pas was the first warning signal to conservatives that McCain might have overplayed his hand.

But Governor Palin's appeal to the Republican right wing was undeniable. Her chief function, according to American Studies Professor Robert Schmuhl from the University of Notre Dame, was to "rally the base which had always been somewhat suspicious of John McCain". The Arizona senator had come this far without the full backing of the far right, and even with

Palin by his side, elements in the Republican Party were still giving him the cold shoulder.

"TOM DELAY?" I ASKED, AS I STEPPED towards a smallish man being fenced off a by a gaggle of young political operatives in kitten heels. "Yes," he smiled. I had barely said "I'm from Ireland" when he grabbed my hand and pressed my palm so hard that I had to pry it loose. "I'm off to Dublin to receive a 'Hammer' award," the Texan gushed, anxious that I hear all the details. Until 2006, Tom DeLay was one of the best-known faces in American politics. A fierce Bush loyalist, DeLay was nicknamed "The Hammer" for his take-no-prisoners approach to marshalling support for President Bush's policies as House Majority leader. But then Republicans lost their majority in the House of Representatives, and DeLay was toppled amidst allegations of money laundering. Trinity College Dublin, it seemed, had noticed DeLay's contribution to conservative rule and was planning to honour him.

"What about John McCain?" I asked, expecting the usual predictions of victory in November. "I'm not here for McCain. I'm here to support Sarah Palin," DeLay retorted, claiming that Palin was everything conservatives had been "begging for" for years. "I think it's very exciting that John McCain, who does not like hardcore conservatives, could very well be responsible for Governor Palin being president some day."

John McCain, in fact, did not favour hardcore conservatives and had once called the religious broadcasters Jerry Falwell and Pat Robertson "agents of intolerance". Senator McCain loathed petty arguments about gay marriage and privacy issues, but he feared that without a running mate who openly embraced God and guns, the hard right would stay at home in

2008. "I know McCain. He doesn't like that crowd," said *Boston Globe* columnist Kevin Cullen. "But like all politicians, he's had to say things and do things he doesn't genuinely believe to get elected."

I still wondered how Tom DeLay could support Sarah Palin but not John McCain. Clearly Palin was the sweetener that would make the bad medicine go down. "I'll vote for McCain, because I don't want Obama," DeLay said, describing Barack Obama as one of the most "radical socialists" ever to run for president. With an upcoming Democratic Congress, DeLay was petrified that President Barack Obama would "set the nation back fifty years".

I was soon reminded that in America God leans Republican. Here's how you can tell. Take the political platforms of both parties and ask which conforms to the Bible. If you have any familiarity with the Good Book, the answer is obvious. Republican policies are in lock step with the word of God, while Democratic positions are hopelessly out of whack.

Dressed in Katharine Hepburn-styled pants, the elegant Texan woman who briefed me on this was ready to go beyond cultural issues such as abortion and gay marriage to unearth biblical justification for low taxes, self-reliance and the whole nine yards. I had simply inquired as to why she was a Republican and did not expect the Gospel according to St John. But she had her point, and we were just killing time waiting for the Almighty to finish rearranging the convention schedule.

It was the last day of August 2008, and Hurricane Gustav was blowing through the Gulf of Mexico like a beast out of hell. Packing winds of 140 miles an hour, Gustav barrelled across Cuba and aimed its evil eye towards, of all places, New Orleans. The roads out of that unfortunate city were crammed with people fleeing the possibility of another disaster. Anyone choosing to stay and protect what they had painstakingly rebuilt since Hurricane Katrina was taking their life in their hands.

For Republicans, the destruction of New Orleans three years earlier had been a political calamity. The flooding of entire sections of the city and the tragic loss of 1,800 lives occurred against a backdrop of glaring government ineptitude and detachment. While the Republican platform has always stressed pulling oneself up by the bootstraps, expecting the poorest to fend for themselves while up to their necks in water was seen as callous and out of touch. A third of the city's population never returned to New Orleans.

When Gustav threatened a repeat performance that would coincide with the first day of the Republican convention in Minnesota, God handed John McCain a chance to make amends. Taking full advantage, the Republican nominee postponed the traditional convention opening, replacing it with a day of prayer and charitable fundraising. It was the stand-out instance during the 2008 campaign where the former naval officer was a man in command of his ship.

Not only did John McCain show that he would not stand for repetition of the mistakes of Hurricane Katrina, he also pushed Vice-President Dick Cheney and President Bush overboard. Both were due to speak at the convention's opening night. Mr Cheney never climbed back on to the schedule and was not seen again before the November election, and George Bush was confined to a long-distance video appearance. In fact, McCain's nomination convention barely acknowledged members of the Bush White House – treating them like a bunch of crazy relatives the family kept locked in the basement.

Having spent the previous week with Democrats, the Republican convention was a totally different kettle of fish. Security in St Paul was lower, crowds smaller and the atmosphere less stressful. Ethnically, too, it could have been another country. Whereas Denver was an eclectic mix of black, white and Hispanic faces, St Paul looked like an Irish ard fheis. Ninety per cent of Republican delegates were white, and seven out of ten were men. Instead of reflecting the nation where minorities will soon be in the majority, the Republican gathering had the feel of a Scots-Irish family reunion.

"Blacks turned their backs on the Republican Party, not the other way around," insisted Frances Rice, chairwoman of the National Black Republican Association, when I asked her about the striking disparity. Rice, a retired army colonel in an impeccably tailored bright red suit, was on a mission to bring black Americans back to their Republican roots. Martin Luther King had been a Republican, and it was Democrats, Rice claimed, who had fought the Civil War to keep slavery alive. As she saw it, the "failed socialism" of the modern Democratic Party had caused untold harm to African-Americans. By supporting Barack Obama, as over 90 per cent would do, she felt blacks were digging themselves deeper into a hole. "He is a far left radical, who should not be president of this country," Frances Rice insisted.

Hispanics too had seemingly drifted away from the Republican base. Though the once revered election strategist Karl Rove had brought in 45 per cent of them for George W. Bush in 2000 and 2004, Latinos looked as if they were moving on. "The Republican base is very hostile to illegal immigration, and that rubbed Hispanics up the wrong way," said Peter Beinart of the Council on Foreign Relations. Once Hispanics became middle class, Beinart felt, they would eventually shift back to the Republicans – like many of the Irish, Italians and Poles had done.

Back in the convention centre – before anyone could get a measure of the dynamic "Hockey Mom" who balanced "a breast pump in one hand and a Blackberry in the other" – news emerged that Sarah Palin was about to be a grandmother. The revelation was mild, however, compared to the rumours swirling for hours around St Paul that Trig, her five-month-old baby boy, might be Bristol Palin's child. Sarah Palin's seventeen-year-old daughter had missed several months of school the previous year, and internet gossips had cooked up a plot which required us to believe that Governor Palin had faked a pregnancy to protect Bristol. The chinwags were mistaken, but they were on to something. To calm the growing hysteria, McCain's Truth Squad had no choice but to make the Palin predicament public knowledge. Within hours, Bristol Palin's was the most talked about teen pregnancy since Jamie Lynn Spears.

Far from raising the ire of the conservative right, as teen pregnancies usually do, the response from even the most ardent family values advocates was sympathetic. So long as Bristol Palin was keeping her baby, the development would not derail her mother's onward march to Washington. James Dobson, whose conservative interest group Focus on the Family had spent a lifetime decrying the decline of family values, took a pass on the pre-marital sex lectures and said that Palin and her family were "only human". Another group, The Family Research Council, praised Alaska's First Family for "choosing life in the midst of a difficult situation".

What raised more heckles than the pregnancy was the suggestion that Sarah Palin should stay at home and look after her children. "The possibility of our vice-president being a mother of five is ridiculous," wrote Deirdre Carrell from Berryville, Virginia, in a letter to *The Washington Post*. "Is motherhood not rewarding enough for Sarah Palin?"

"We wouldn't be asking a man that question," fumed a self-described "Hockey Mom" back at the convention in St Paul. But an emerging debate about Palin's ability to balance her roles as a mother and as a national figure quickly fizzled when the McCain campaign challenged CNN and other media outlets to back off. Such a swift and effective backlash against the more liberal media was something that Hillary Clinton had never benefited from. But, for Sarah Palin, it was to be short-lived.

Amidst all this, President Bush's video address to the Republican convention was reminiscent of the "boy in the bubble". "John is an independent man who thinks for himself," the President declared from a large screen above the convention stage – from where it was hoped he could not infect candidate McCain with a dose of Bush's historically low ratings. "He's not afraid to tell you when he disagrees," the President said.

In pointing out their differences, Bush gave McCain some distance. On the few occassions in 2008 that George Bush was allowed to speak, the lame duck president said whatever it took to help the Republican nominee – even if it meant pretending they had nothing in common. But opposition researchers are paid to find good sound bites, and the bite of John McCain saying he had agreed with George W. Bush's policies "95 per cent of the time" was as good as anything the Democrats had ever uncovered. They used it repeatedly.

By late 2008, just two out of ten Americans claimed to support President Bush. I met most of them in St Paul. The Republican Party faithful, who had nominated a Bush for either president or vice-president in six of the past seven elections stretching back to 1980, remained so loyal that they could not see why John McCain needed to keep George W. Bush at arm's length.

"I love the man," declared a tall Texan in khaki shorts, who claimed to be privy to a stack of insider stories from the president's Secret Service agents. "Did you know that he can remember a person's name and face and what they talk about for five years?" he asked, claiming that most Americans had not appreciated George Bush's true intelligence. "He can recite the Bible from memory," the Texan added.

"I honour President Bush for drawing a line in the sand and keeping us safe at home," said Stacy Fenton, who felt America had enjoyed seven good years under George W. Bush. In 2007, Stacy's son-in-law Coby Schwab was killed by a roadside bomb while serving in Ramadi, Iraq. Yet Fenton still supported the war. Sheryl Sheaffer wore three military dog tags around her neck as a way of keeping her own sons close while they fought the unpopular war. It was the US Congress and not George Bush who sent them to Iraq, Sheaffer believed. "But if you are the figurehead, you get all the blame," she said, claiming that Bush unfairly shouldered the brunt of the backlash.

It was true that Donald Rumsfeld, the former Defence Secretary who helped frame US policy in Guantanamo Bay and in Iraqi and prisons, had escaped the worst of the criticism by resigning early. I spotted Paul Wolfowitz, another key member of the Bush foreign policy team, on the street in St Paul, but if he was there for the Republican convention he too kept a low profile.

As military mothers running a support group for soldiers at war, these women were genuinely spooked by the idea of

Barack Obama as Commander-in-Chief. "Our troops tell us they won't serve under Obama," Sheaffer's mother Nadine said, claiming that Obama's plan to reduce the size of the military would make life more dangerous for the soldiers. Democrats "call themselves anti-war, but it's anti-military," she declared.

Though Barack Obama had never outlined any plan to reduce the size of the military and had actually talked about increasing its size, the women's minds were made up. "He has not put his country first long enough to understand the ins and outs of diplomacy and dealing with terrorist nations," insisted Sheryl Sheaffer. "That worries me."

Having spent months talking to both Democrats and Republicans, I realised that both groups were better at explaining what they were voting *against* than what they were voting *for*. Democrats planned to repudiate the past – two deadly wars, economic decline and the loss of international prestige. That was a given. But the Republican base was also emerging as a fighting force designed to reject a bleak future for an America dominated by the twin evils of socialism and far-left liberalism. Though known in his youth as "McNasty", seventy-two-year-old John McCain was not particularly adept at this type of partisan scaremongering. But "Super Sarah" had no problem in firing off a good zinger. As with many couples, he made the snowballs and she threw them.

The moment Palin appeared on stage at the Republican convention, it was obvious that the governor was undaunted by the personal trials of her rapid rise to national prominence. Far from it, the perky woman, conservatively dressed in a black skirt and high-necked jacket, relished the idea of tackling the largest audience of her life. Wearing her trademark glasses and hair down to her shoulders, Sarah Palin was itching to get going. A record forty million Americans tuned in and won Palin more viewers than Barack Obama had drawn for his much-hyped closing speech the previous week at Denver's football stadium.

"I was just your average hockey mom and signed up to the PTA because I wanted to make my kids' public education better," Palin said, introducing herself as one who had begun without political ambition. Sarah Palin was playing to the "American Idol" audience, the millions of American women who might look at her and say, "Maybe that could be me". Palin's intention was that her story, as the mother of both a Down's syndrome child and a pregnant teenager, as well as the wife of an oil worker, would make women feel as though she could be their voice in the White House.

But Governor Palin was more than just an ordinary mom. She had energy, ambition and the instincts of an attack dog. "The difference between a hockey mom and a Pit Bull?" Palin asked with a smile. "Lipstick!" This gutsy punch line was the beginning of Palin-mania, a phenomenon that blossomed and grew as she pulled even bigger crowds to Republican rallies than the presidential nominee himself.

From the start, Sarah Palin drew out battle lines for the forthcoming race. She was for voters in America's small towns who "grow our food, run our factories and fight our wars". She was against the media and the so-called "Washington elite" who had begun to pick apart her résumé and her record. "Here's a little news flash for all those reporters and commentators. I'm not going to Washington to seek their good opinion. I'm going to Washington to serve the people of this country!" Palin announced, drawing wild applause from the Republican base. The elderly Republican couple standing next to me kept missing Palin's best lines. When I repeated them into their ears, the two hollered as if they had won the Mega Millions lottery.

But on the night of her national debut, Governor Sarah Palin reserved her real "Pit Bull" instincts for Barack Obama. "I guess a small town mayor is sort of like a 'community organiser' except that you have actual responsibilities," she said, referring to Obama's work on Chicago's South Side. The gibe had a caustic edge to it, and Palin was not done attacking the Democratic nominee. "We have all heard his dramatic speeches before devoted followers, and there is much to admire about our opponent. But listening to him speak, it's easy to forget that this is a man who has authored two memoirs but not a single major law or reform."

The old couple beside me were ecstatic again. If there had been shots of whiskey lined up in front of them, they would have been knocking them back.

Palin worked the base to a fever pitch. By the end, she had painted a picture of a heroic reformer who had rejected an Alaskan project, called the "Bridge to Nowhere", that would have cost American taxpayers over $200 million, and who had sold the governor's jet on eBay. To my ears, Palin's was the most riveting speech of the convention season, and John McCain looked like Henry Higgins after he took Eliza Doolittle to the ball.

"She is going to bring this party up," cooed Linda Buckles of the Tennessee Women's Federation. "The gloves are off!" agreed Shirley Ward, warning that Democrats were in for some "real good competition now".

Among older female voters, Sarah Palin was already doing what Hillary Clinton had done for the Democrats – offering pensioners like Janet Doran from Tennessee the hope that in their lifetime they might see a woman in the White House. "We are far more overdue than the black men in this country," Doran claimed. "She's perfect," gushed a delegate from Georgia. "She's pro-life, and she's a shooter!" the woman said, seconding Palin's choice to see human life as sacred and animals as food.

"Game on," senior McCain adviser Steve Schmidt said to fellow staffers after Palin's performance. Matthew Scully, who rewrote Palin's speech from a draft she had prepared for another occasion, was treated to a standing ovation from campaign colleagues at their Minneapolis hotel that evening.

Former Presidential candidate Mike Huckabee must have wondered how he had missed the train. "It elevates women in our party," he told me with a broad smile, but in a less frantic electoral environment it might have been him up there wowing the base. Huckabee had all Sarah Palin's conservative credentials, and as a two-term Arkansas governor he was vastly more experienced. But lipstick was all the rage now. It just didn't suit him.

One week into her campaign, 40 per cent of Americans believed Sarah Palin was more qualified to lead America than Barack Obama. That was a jolt to Obama, who had been slogging it out on the national scene and silencing audiences with his oratory for eighteen months. Nothing, however, could change the fact that Senator Obama had not governed a state, a small town, or even run a sweet shop. Rhetoric could only take him so far, and latent racism was a potential threat to his steadfast ambition. Obama was banking on intellect, character and a repudiation of the Bush era to take him to the White House.

Near the convention centre, the man trying to drum up a presidential scandal did not look like Barack Obama's type.

Larry Sinclair – a short, pasty-faced, pot-bellied man – was sweating in the afternoon sun and worn out from shouting into a megaphone. Sinclair wanted passers-by to know that he had done crack cocaine with Obama in the back of a limousine. Not only that, Sinclair alleged, Obama had a history of gay sexual encounters in Chicago. He held up a photo of an alleged lover, a dreadlocked African-American named Donald Young, who looked to be in his early twenties. And where was he now? "Gunned down execution-style on the streets of Chicago in November of 2007." Either this was a cracking yarn, or the man with the loudhailer was still high on something. "Why has nobody reported it?" I inquired, fishing a fresh notebook from my bag and drawing a bit of a crowd in the process. "The mainstream media won't touch it," Sinclair said, handing me a business card complete with phone numbers and a website address where I could assess the evidence for myself.

"You're media, aren't you?" asked an onlooker, nodding to me as though he expected me to start barking lines of copy down the phone to an excited news editor on the other end. "I can back this all up," Sinclair added helpfully. "Oh, go on! I'm not voting for Obama anyway," shrieked a woman eager for Sinclair to spill the goods on the Democratic nominee. A man in a suit entered the circle and angrily challenged Sinclair to admit that he was peddling a pack of lies.

"There's a whole website full of alleged gay lovers," the man shouted, waving his arms to scatter the crowd. Larry Sinclair was aware of internet impostors but was sticking to his story. "Republicans are probably paying him to do it," the irate intruder suggested, as we all backed away, leaving Sinclair to begin his pitch to a fresh group of gawping onlookers. As the dog-eat-dog election entered its final phase, Sinclair's was just one of hundreds of bizarre stories circulating around the perimeters of both party conventions.

A LOT OF THE FUN AT CONVENTIONS happens off camera. What ends up on the evening news is highly scripted and rehearsed. In these days of micromanaged campaigns, candidates' speeches are ghostwritten by individuals paid to come up with punch lines, and cheerleaders stand in the aisles to tell delegates how and when to react.

On the afternoon of his acceptance speech, John McCain tried the podium for size and took a turn at the teleprompter. Behind McCain, his ninety-six-year-old mother Roberta and wife Cindy chatted with floor managers. "What happened to your arm?" we shouted to Cindy, who sported a bright pink cast. "I've been shaking too many hands," she replied. Unlike Michelle Obama, who only joined her husband for major events, Cindy McCain was a permanent fixture beside her husband on the campaign trail. Though a true humanitarian who has done much for charities, Mrs McCain frequently appeared in haute couture outfits and expensive jewellery – a choice that sent a jarring message to a nation quickly sinking into recession. That night in St Paul, *Vanity Fair* calculated that her ensemble, including diamonds, was valued at $300,000.

"I hate war," John McCain declared, when he finally accepted his nomination. These were arresting words from a man who favoured remaining in Iraq "for one hundred years if necessary", but the Arizona senator had a story to tell:

> "When I was five years old, a car pulled up in front of our house. A Navy officer rolled down the window, and shouted at my father that the Japanese had bombed Pearl Harbor. I rarely saw my father again for four years. My

grandfather came home from that same war, exhausted from the burdens he had borne, and died the next day. In Vietnam, where I formed the closest friendships of my life, some of those friends never came home with me. I hate war. It is terrible beyond imagination."

Though the senator did not explode any shells in attacking his opponent, John McCain argued he would be the real agent of change in Washington DC. If it was "change" Americans wanted, he urged them to do more than just talk about it:

"If you find faults with our country, make it a better one. If you're disappointed with the mistakes of government, join its ranks and work to correct them. Enlist in our armed forces. Become a teacher. Enter the ministry. Run for public office. Feed a hungry child. Stand up for each other; for beautiful, blessed, bountiful America. Stand up, stand up, stand up and fight. Nothing is inevitable here. We're Americans, and we never give up. We never quit. We never hide from history. We make history."

By the second week of September 2008, Republican themes for the final push had been set. A McCain-Palin administration would keep taxes low to stimulate the economy, bring America's soldiers home from Iraq only as winners, and make oil drilling a great national cause. With disdain for both elitism and business-as-usual, John McCain and Sarah Palin presented themselves as champions of small-town folks. It wasn't the worst strategy, but events were about to overtake them. A "September Surprise" was in the works, and the 2008 election would belong not only to small town folks but to all Americans.

ST PAUL IS JUST A FEW MILES EAST from its twin city of Minneapolis. On that city's college campus along the northern reach of the Mississippi River, the more diverse young population made the Republicans look like an old-fashioned cult from out on the prairies. That day, my No. 16 bus – which ran between St Paul and the University of Minnesota in Minneapolis – was more of an urban experience than the college itself. The bus was filled with black teenagers, Muslim women in head-scarves, Indian students, and young Spanish- and Chinese-speakers. We rode past Islamic centres, Oriental health shops, and an old car on the roadside from which two black men were selling Obama t-shirts. The teens talked about how Obama might make a "great president". In all likelihood, there was not a single John McCain voter on the No. 16 bus.

Truth be told, many passengers that afternoon were probably among the fifty per cent of Americans who have historically failed to show up for elections, but by the autumn of 2008, many had already encountered one of the thousands of volunteers registering new voters and been convinced to fill out an application. Maybe an extra five to ten per cent of Americans would find time to go to the polls in November. And once in the booth, they would cast a vote for an idea that had become embedded in their minds. Their lives might change – if not directly, then indirectly – by empowering a minority candidate like themselves. In 2008, these new young voters *were* the change Barack Obama envisioned.

13

Meltdown

"I think we need a generational change.... I'll be voting for Senator Barack Obama." – FORMER SECRETARY OF STATE COLIN POWELL

THE WORST FINANCIAL MELTDOWN since the Great Depression struck on a Sunday evening in September 2008. It came in the guise of Lehman Brothers, and the news was that the brothers were gone. A once revered investment bank, a pillar of Wall Street, had collapsed – just like that. We scratched our heads. We tuned into our televisions. But we did not fully comprehend it. No regrets were expressed as staff left Lehman's New York headquarters with their belongings in cardboard boxes. It must have been their own fault. The "fat cats" must have robbed the place blind.

By the following morning, the rot had spread and America's largest insurance company was gasping for breath. On the business channels, new terms like "credit default swap" and "derivatives" rolled off the tongues of talking heads as if they had known about them all along. "Very risky, a house of cards, a day of reckoning..." they said. No one seemed stunned, except ordinary taxpayers, small stock investors and former Federal Reserve Chairman Alan Greenspan, who for nineteen years had appeared on Capitol Hill as the undisputed expert on the American economy.

Hunched over his papers before lawmakers, Greenspan would rattle off strings of financial jargon. "Not only have individual financial institutions become less vulnerable to shocks from underlying risk factors, but also the financial system as a whole has become more resilient," he opined in 2004. Nobody ever really knew what Greenspan's mumbo jumbo meant, but few questioned the man they called "the Oracle". As it turned out, Alan Greenspan was a fan of the risky investment vehicles that helped to bring the house down in the autumn of 2008. He argued against tying them up in regulations. For two decades, Greenspan and others promoted "faith in the market" and in the men and women who ran it. But in October 2008, the eighty-two-year-old admitted he had been "mistaken".

By week one of the Wall Street crisis, residents in Annapolis, Maryland, were panicked about their savings. "I just came from the bank trying to transfer money in case something happens," a thin blonde girl said, blaming the scare on those who had taken out housing loans they could no longer afford.

At least she *had* a savings account to worry about. Many Americans are heavily invested in their homes or in the stock market, and both these took a severe beating in 2008. "It will take six years for families to achieve the financial security they had at the end of 2007," estimated Christian Weller of the Center for American Progress Action Fund in Washington DC. Weller disagreed that the crisis had been caused by Americans living beyond their means. Since 2001, he said, ordinary families had fallen further into debt because of stagnant wages, plus a jump in the cost of housing and health care. "Years ago, it would be hard to imagine a medical emergency putting someone into debt," Weller said. Now, the accumulated unpaid bills from one serious illness can "bankrupt an American family".

With talk of another Great Depression, some parents removed children from private schools, abandoned vacations and restricted shopping to sale items. "I shop with newspaper coupons only," a young mother said, as she wheeled a huge trolley of groceries to her car in the initial week of the meltdown. She was happy to have no debts. It was the average person owing $12,000 on their credit cards that she was praying for.

In a country that depends on continual shopping for about three-quarters of its economic activity, this belt-tightening by citizens was already causing job losses, and by late 2008 America's unemployment rate had approached 7 per cent. American Express, DHL and General Motors were among the big names forced to cut thousands of jobs. The owner of a small Annapolis car repair shop was not looking forward to laying off any of his twelve employees, but he knew it would not be long. "Normally I have them working all day – busy from seven in the morning until five. Lately, they have been running out of work at noon," he said, adding that customers were not getting their cars serviced as frequently as they used to.

There was more bad news at the church where for three years I have volunteered with the St Vincent de Paul Society. Eric Brown, chairman of the Annapolis Housing Authority, was evicting those who had failed to pay the meagre amount of rent levied by the public housing system. "We really try to work with them, but we have twelve hundred people on waiting lists to get into these houses," Brown said. For every home that became available, there were 400 Annapolis families waiting to take occupancy.

Volunteering at St Mary's, I saw workers squeezed tighter from 2007 to 2008. Electricity bills doubled, food prices shot up, and the spike in the cost of petrol ate into family budgets. People who never dreamt they would need charity showed up at our door, looking for help to clear their mounting debts. On some days, the lines of those seeking assistance were longer than we could deal with in the allotted time.

The first to appear were generally the young African-American mothers, nursing assistants or cashiers earning $10 to $12 an hour, almost double the minimum wage of $6.50. Yet in 2008, nobody got by on one of those jobs. After tax, take home pay was about $1,400 a month. But once rent, electricity, medical expenses, car insurance and petrol were paid, there was no more than $150-300 remaining to feed the family for a month. Most of the women were single mothers caring for children whose fathers had either left or been imprisoned. A little extra, borrowed from a sympathetic relative, usually tided them over from one week to the next. But when that failed, the mothers held their heads high and did the rounds of the local churches.

Wall Street, it could be said, loaded the gun on the "September Surprise" but the housing market was the trigger. The ownership society heavily promoted by both the Clinton and Bush administrations was a policy aimed at putting more Americans into their own homes. "No Document" and "No Income, No Job and No Assets" or NINJA loans, vigorously dispensed by banks and immediately sold on to investment houses and brokers, facilitated the madness. When the borrowers at the bottom of the pyramid scheme defaulted, the system came undone.

Passing the Anne Arundel County Courthouse, I stopped to listen to real estate auctioneers engaged in the bizarre outdoor ritual of the disposal of homes that had fallen on the foreclosure pyre. By the courthouse door, bargain hunters stood talking into mobile phones as auctioneers called out over the noise of street traffic. "The bank bids $315,000 for 1544 Palm Court. Any advance on $315,000?" shouted auctioneer Andrew Schechter one Monday morning. He had no takers. "Twice at 315. Three times." The house went back to the bank.

Foreclosed homes sold on the courthouse steps could not be viewed before purchase, but it was well known that many were vandalised by owners as a parting shot to the banks and lenders who had roped them into the sorry mess. Windows were sometimes smashed, light fittings removed and food left rotting in kitchens. Some defaulting owners simply threw the keys in the letter box and walked away – giving rise to the term "jingle mail".

The owner of 1544 Palm Court had barely made the first couple of payments before defaulting, Schechter said. "Is it depressing?" I asked him, given that behind each of these sales was a family who had to leave a dream home. "It's my job," Schechter replied. "It's how I feed my family."

Even as America's so-called credit crunch deepened, fresh opportunities to fall into debt kept coming in the door. "Save hundreds of dollars on high-rate balances when you transfer them to our No Hassle Gold MasterCard" was how one bank offered to take over your credit card debt. During September and October 2008, as trillions of dollars were erased from the total wealth of ordinary consumers, countless Americans continued to be pre-approved for an average of two new credit cards per week. Go figure. Keep spending.

Shopping without money is a quirk of American life I have never grown accustomed to. With my Macy's card, I can shop at the vast department store and take away bagloads of new clothes without seeing a bill for months. After eight years here, the "No Money Down" offers on items ranging from coats to cars still make me feel as though I am engaged in a form of looting.

"Credit or debit?" asked the teenage cashier at the local supermarket, where I was picking up milk, a loaf of bread and a few other items totaling less than nine dollars one morning. "Cash," I replied, handing over a $10 bill. "Cash?" she repeated loudly, her eyes widening. "Nobody uses that any more!" For a minute, I wasn't sure if she even knew what to do with it.

By the third week of September, the US government had gone into both the mortgage and insurance businesses – the result of having bailed out Fannie Mae, Freddie Mac and AIG – all private companies serving tens of millions of Americans. "Congratulations, taxpayers. You are now the proud owner of an insurance company," *The Washington Post* announced, heralding what many saw as the privatisation of profit and the socialisation of debt. But there was worse to come. "Credit squeeze" had become "credit freeze". Banks had stopped lending, so to unblock the system, Treasury Secretary Henry Paulson, a vague and unfamiliar figure to most Americans, proposed a $700 billion rescue package known as TARP or the Troubled Asset Relief Program. Paulson was now clearly calling the shots in Washington. President Bush, who looked as if he was afraid of being stoned if he came farther than the Rose Garden, called on Congress to support the bailout package. But each time Bush spoke, the markets took another dive.

THE BATTLE FOR THE WHITE HOUSE found its feet amidst the financial turmoil. Bill Clinton's old adage that "It's the economy, stupid!" never seemed more appropriate. As the repercussions spread from Wall Street to Main Street, Americans glimpsed how both John McCain and Barack Obama would operate in a crisis.

For Senator McCain, it was his impetuous streak that caught hold as he boldly placed his next gamble. The Republican candidate abruptly suspended his election campaign and suggested postponing the first presidential debate set for the following weekend. "Is it because the economy is sliding or his poll numbers are sliding?" asked television talk show host David Letterman, who was due to interview McCain but who had been informed that the Senator was "racing back to Washington" to deal with the economic meltdown. "This isn't the way a tested hero behaves!" mocked Letterman, suggesting that his old friend McCain was panicking.

John McCain had already admitted his weak background on economic issues. "I don't know as much about the economy as I should," he commented during the primaries. The middle-class, he once claimed, were those earning "less than five million", but his failure to recall how many homes he owned was a far more damaging blow to his presidential hopes. "I'll have my staff get back to you," McCain told reporters, casting him as greatly out of touch with ordinary citizens who faced plummeting house values and foreclosure.

The McCains reportedly owned at least seven properties, including a six-acre ranch in Arizona and condominiums in Virginia and California, most of them in wife Cindy McCain's name. In 2008, the family also owned thirteen cars. As the owner of one home and one Ford, Barack Obama was instantly viewed as the leader with a deeper personal understanding of the country's coming economic pain. As the stock market spiralled downwards, Senator McCain's assessment that the economy was "fundamentally sound" left many wondering if the Republican had lost his grip on reality.

Though pocketbook issues took centre stage as the candidates entered the final stretch of the election, voters were fretting about their finances long before the autumn of 2008. "The labour market was the first thing to be hit," said economist Christian Weller, noting that those in the heartland had begun to feel the pain of job losses in 2007. America's once great auto industry was fighting to stay alive, and particularly in Michigan, workers were losing out to foreign competition. As they battled through the primaries, both Hillary Clinton and Barack Obama focused on bringing jobs back home to America. "John McCain paid no attention to the economy until September," said Weller. "Obama had already been out there talking about jobs for several months."

John McCain's attempt to suspend the first presidential debate met with a fiery response from Barack Obama, who was already rehearsing for the showdown. "This is exactly the time when the American people need to hear from the person who will be the next president," Obama said. "It's going to be part of the president's job to deal with more than one thing at once. It's important that we present ourselves to the American public."

That week both candidates joined George Bush in the White House to discuss the $700 billion bailout plan. Reports of the crisis meeting with the President suggested that John McCain remained silent and offered little input. To the contrary, Obama engaged the financial experts and left 1600 Pennsylvania Avenue believing that the package, while flawed, deserved support. Although he knew it would be difficult for conservatives to swallow, John McCain agreed. "Both the Republican base and independent voters despised the bailout bill," said Greg Valliere, chief political strategist with the Stanford Group in Washington. "For McCain to embrace it showed that he's no maverick."

On 26 September, the first presidential debate went ahead as scheduled in Oxford, Mississippi. Throughout, John McCain refused to look directly at Obama and appeared patronising towards his younger opponent as they sparred over foreign policy. "I'm afraid Senator Obama doesn't understand the difference between a tactic and a strategy," McCain said of Obama's decision not to back the surge of extra troops into Iraq in 2007 – which Senator McCain agued had saved Iraq from total chaos. Downplaying the effect of the surge, Senator Obama argued that the Iraq war had not started in 2007 but back in 2003, when the initial mistake to invade was made, a blunder McCain had supported.

The second town hall-style debate in Nashville, Tennessee saw John McCain grow more jittery. The Senator flitted around the stage in a manner described by conservative columnist Peggy Noonan as "a rabbity forest creature darting amid the hedgerows". In a less than presidential gesture, McCain also pointed at Obama, calling him "That One". Refusing to be provoked, Barack Obama flashed a broad smile. He did, however, irk his opponent by reminding him of the time McCain had entertained a group of war veterans by singing, "Ba, Ba, Ba, Bomb, Bomb Iran" to the tune of the Beach Boys hit song "Barbara Ann".

Out on the election trail, it was all Palin, all the time. Since John McCain first introduced the Governor of Alaska to

American voters, they could not get enough of her, and the numbers attending campaign rallies doubled overnight. The mother of five, with her spunky attitude and disdain for the mainstream media, was on a roll. Beyond her beloved Republican base, however, Sarah Palin was falling flat, and declining poll numbers indicated that she was dragging John McCain down with her. "By picking her, it inhibited John McCain from trying to broaden his appeal," said Professor Robert Schmuhl of the University of Notre Dame, who saw McCain lose moderate and independent voters once they decided that Palin was the wrong choice.

By now there were as many journalists as wolves prowling around Alaska, and despite the presence of McCain's message controllers, what emerged was at odds with the self-image Palin had presented as a maverick reformer. Since becoming governor two years earlier, Sarah Palin had spent more than 300 days away from her office in Juneau, Alaska's capital. Preferring to work from her hometown of Wasilla, she reportedly claimed out-of-office expenses for herself and her children. Governor Palin had also conducted official state business on her personal email accounts and relieved some officials of their posts – replacing them with her girlfriends. It was not the profile of a reformer who would clean up Washington DC.

Back on the trail, handlers played with Palin's personal appearance. Republican National Committee funds estimated at $150,000 were spent on makeup and a new wardrobe to smarten her up, plus a travelling hairstylist at a cost of $20,000 a month. When the price of the makeover was publicised, Sarah Palin claimed to have returned the clothes to the RNC – saying she would have preferred a few items from her favourite Alaskan consignment store. Some felt the RNC should have kept the money and given Palin a copy of the US Constitution outlining the role of the vice-president. Instead, Governor Palin was given two thick folders of "talking points" to study and directed to speak to handpicked reporters only – one of many restrictions she later criticised.

Palin's unfamiliarity with affairs beyond the borders of her home state quickly became her biggest problem. Her claim that she would be comfortable negotiating with Russia because "you can actually see Russia from some land here in Alaska" was greeted with howls of derision. News that she had obtained a passport just two years earlier and made only one trip abroad to visit Alaskan troops in Kuwait – with a stopover in Shannon – did not enhance her vice-presidential credentials. "The lack of intellectual curiosity of this woman was what was shocking to me, the more I found out about it," said Kevin Cullen, a columnist with the *Boston Globe*. "She really did remind me of George Bush." With the chance of McCain dying in office and Palin replacing him, Cullen was among those who felt Palin's candidacy deserved more press scrutiny than Joe Biden's. "I don't want to sit in my house and think I'm smarter than the president of the United States," Cullen said, adding that it seemed as though the conservative movement had been hijacked in recent years by an "anti-intellectual" element.

Saturday Night Live, the comedy show that had earlier pilloried Hillary Clinton, soon got to work on Sarah Palin. Bearing an uncanny resemblance to Palin, actress Tina Fey drew record audiences simply by using scripts of Palin's actual answers to journalists' questions. Palin meandered frequently into the Twilight Zone, such as when asked if global warming was real. "You know, there are man's activities that can be contributed to the issues that we're dealing with now – these impacts. I'm not going to solely blame all of man's activities on changes in climate, because the world's weather patterns are cyclical. And over history, we have seen changes there. But it kind of doesn't matter, at this point, as we debate what caused it." Commentators, both liberal and conservative, concluded that should anything happen to the seventy-two-year-old John McCain in office, Sarah Palin was not ready to be president.

"Some tulip alright, that bird!" was the assessment of a Dublin taxi driver I spoke to while on a quick trip back to Ireland in the autumn of 2008. The taxi man had followed Palin's progress and couldn't see her making it to the White House. The more experienced Hillary Clinton had been his choice for president. However, Dubliner Frank Corrigan felt that Palin was a winning addition to the Republican ticket. "A real breath of fresh air," he said, predicting that Palin would put John McCain over the top.

The sole debate match-up between Joe Biden and Sarah Palin in St Louis, Missouri attracted a record 70 million viewers – more than the presidential debates themselves. Curiosity about Sarah Palin peaked, as many waited for her train to come off the tracks. Unable to locate a Palin party, I tuned in with a group of Obama supporters at election headquarters in Severna Park, Maryland. Democrats of all ages and races gathered to watch the night's debate – including African-American women who passed out salads and corn bread, kids in pyjamas, plus a teenage boy called JT who took the names and numbers of those willing to canvass door-to-door for Obama. As Joe Biden and Sarah Palin came on stage, we were handed sheets of "Palin Bingo" – a game that involved marking off key words such Alaska, Maverick and Hockey Mom as Palin uttered them.

"She's going down!" shouted a white man to my right, as Sarah Palin wrestled with an answer on foreign policy. Palin had studied her position on Iran and Iraq, holding her own against the more experienced Joe Biden. But her tendency to revert to personal experiences as a small town mayor whenever she was stuck drew jeers from the assembled Democrats. "Here's my world view," Sarah Palin began in answer to a debate question. "And what would that be, honey?" a prim black woman, dressed as though for church, retorted from the front of our room. Everyone giggled. While these Obama supporters clearly adhered to a more liberal worldview, they were not the elites Palin sought to bypass in addressing her answers to "all you Hockey Moms and Joe Six-Packs out there".

"Bingo!" JT cried out. Palin had hit her quota of clichés but was still standing. She might not have bested long-time Senator Joe Biden, but by the end of the night Palin remained in the game. "I thought she was going to do a terrible job and crash the campaign, but she was able to take Biden on," said JT afterwards. Mike Miller, who organised the debate party, was less impressed. "She demonstrates a remarkable ignorance of things like the Constitution," Miller said. "She was coached," another man commented. "I wouldn't trust her as vice-president." As for Palin's targeted demographic, Joe Six-Pack, the Severna Park Democrats claimed that back in Ireland he would likely be "Joe Guinness".

Regardless of her knowledge of the issues, Governor Palin's willingness to play hardball was no longer in doubt. Weeks out from the election, she reopened an old line of attack against Obama and accused him of "palling around with terrorists" like William Ayers. Partisan Republicans, genuinely wary of Senator Obama, were delighted. William Ayers had founded an anti-war group in the 1960s called the Weathermen, which had carried out a series of bombings in public buildings. Now an education professor in Chicago, Ayers had once sat on the same charitable board as Obama. Quickly reacting to Palin's new stump line, Senator Obama said he condemned Ayers' "despicable acts", carried out "when I was eight years old". With Ayers on the table, however, Palin's rallies took on an angry tone. Racial slurs were heard at rallies, and in Florida a Palin supporter – referring to Obama – shouted "Kill him!"

On a near-freezing Saturday morning in Lancaster, Pennsylvania, I lined up with 8,000 Republicans to see Sarah Palin work a crowd. Lancaster is in the heart of Amish country, a Republican area where farming, religion and traditional family values dominate. Approaching the security checkpoint, I saw people wearing t-shirts that said "Read My Lipstick", "Pitt Bulls for Palin" and "Nobama".

"She's one of us," said Tom Mack, an elderly man who had been in line since 7 a.m. "Very sincere. Puts God first."

Inside the baseball stadium, Sarah Palin walked down a long ramp to the tune of "Isn't She Lovely?" Oblivious to the cold, she wore a short black skirt and high boots, and in her arms she carried her baby son Trig wrapped in a snowsuit. "This feels cosy to me," the Alaskan commented about the weather, before handing the child off to a waiting aide.

Palin's theme for the day was Barack Obama's plan to raise taxes for businesses making over $250,000 a year. "Barack Obama wants to spread your wealth around. That sounds a lot like socialism to me," Palin said to loud applause and chants of "Sarah! Sarah!" Her description of the Democratic tax plan as "socialism" was the Republican's final line of attack and probably their most successful, thanks largely to a tall, bald-headed Ohio man known as "Joe the Plumber".

"Joe the Plumber", who had challenged Barack Obama at a rally in Ohio, shot to stardom when John McCain brought him into the Republican campaign as the "No New Taxes" guy. Joe, whose real name is Sam, did not have a proper plumber's licence and showed his distaste for taxes by not fully paying them, but in Joe the Republicans had found a working man whose views resonated with voters. In Lancaster a middle-aged construction contractor, carrying a "Joe the Plumber" placard, predicted he would have to lay off workers if Obama raised taxes. "A small business that makes $250,000 today, that's not wealthy. That's somebody working hard creating jobs for other people," he said, adding that Obama would be redistributing his hard-earned dollars as social welfare.

"It's a dictatorship!" shouted a woman listening nearby. Before I knew it, about a dozen people were gathered around my radio microphone angrily venting their objections to an Obama presidency. "Anyone who talks to Ayers and has a connection with him, I don't want him to be my president," a man yelled, urging others to join him in attacking Obama. "We have a right to know what that man was doing," agreed Lancaster's Monica Fort, who was highly suspicious of the Democratic candidate. "He does not salute the flag. He does not believe in God. He doesn't even put his hand on the Bible for oath. If the Muslims love him, go back there and stay the hell out of America."

"There's an element of the campaign that's so offensive," said Michael Carey, an *Anchorage Daily News* columnist, who claimed that the tenor of Palin's rallies surprised many back home in Alaska. The initial decision to link Barack Obama to William Ayers, Carey believed, unleashed a "nasty" element that could not be undone. As infighting began in Senator McCain's failing campaign, arguments surfaced over whether or not Palin's "palling around with terrorists" line had even been cleared for use by Republican headquarters. John McCain seemed caught between advisers who felt that attacking Obama's character was legitimate and others who felt it damaged McCain's bid for the White House. "McCain needs to connect himself to the middle class. That would be better than character attacks," said strategist Mike Murphy, noting that the American middle ground was shifting towards Obama. By mid-October, the Democratic nominee had large leads in previously Red states, including Virginia, Ohio, Florida, Indiana and Colorado. Insiders in both camps knew that Barack Obama was poised to win the White House.

Against this background, the final presidential debate in Hempstead, New York was make or break for John McCain. He would have to go big on substance and demonstrate leadership. Yet Senator McCain appeared edgy and distracted throughout the ninety-minute debate, clinging to socialism and "Joe the Plumber" as his chief arguments against Obama. In the debate over taxes, however, McCain mentioned Ireland's low corporate tax rate as the way America should be going and rejected suggestions that he was no different from the incumbent president. "I'm not George Bush," McCain told Obama. "If you wanted to run against George Bush, you should have run four years ago," McCain stated to loud cheers.

But when the opportunity arose for John McCain to dispense with slash-and-burn campaigning, he once again linked Barack Obama to William Ayers. Like a schoolyard brawler desperate to throw the last punch, McCain accused Obama of running hundreds of negative ads against him – all of them ostensibly inaccurate. With his eyes darting around nervously, John McCain bounced a pen off his notebook and shifted uncomfortably in his chair until time ran out. This last debate had not been the night he needed.

Senator Barack Obama, having been tutored to remain serious and unflinching, was declared the unofficial winner of all three television debates. Seeing the young Democratic nominee remain calm under pressure allowed wavering voters to become comfortable with the black candidate and, with each confident performance, Obama won new converts. "The debates showed he was a thoughtful person who had worked out his ideas. He was able to present them without any sort of bluster," said Robert Schmuhl of the University of Notre Dame. "He's just a steady figure following a specific strategy." John McCain, Schmuhl felt, appeared "impetuous" in all three debates, as if he would rather be in a dentist's chair.

"If Ronald Reagan himself had been in McCain's chair, there's nothing he could have done," said conservative writer Charles Krauthammer on Fox News after the final debate – all but declaring the game to be over for John McCain. "It's a Democratic year," he said, indicating that all Obama had to do was to look presidential and avoid mistakes. "He's a man of remarkable self-containment. It's his greatest asset," Krauthammer asserted.

As the election entered its final push, a number of conservatives parted company with John McCain. One of the first to defect was Christopher Buckley of *The National Review*, son of its founder, the late William F. Buckley Jr. The younger Buckley endorsed Barack Obama and then submitted his resignation to the *Review*. Kathleen Parker, another writer for the *Review*, suggested dropping Sarah Palin from the ticket. Finally, William

Kristol – known amongst conservatives as the "Pope" – urged John McCain to "junk the whole thing and start over".

None of these stung, however, like the rejection by McCain's long-time friend and senior Republican Colin Powell. "As gifted as he is," Mr Powell said of John McCain, "he is essentially going to execute the Republican agenda with a new face and a maverick approach to it. And he'd be quite good at it. But I think we need a generational change." The former Secretary of State, whose own reputation had been tarnished by the Iraq war, further rebuked Republicans for moving too far right and stated that Sarah Palin was "not ready".

Colin Powell deemed Obama to be a "transformative figure", the type of leader he felt America needed. "I'll be voting for Senator Barack Obama," Powell said.

14

Victory!

"Oh my God! Can you believe it? Oh my God! Oh my God!" – OBAMA SUPPORTER

WITH JUST WEEKS TO GO UNTIL 4 November 2008, Carol Wheeler sounded overworked when she answered the telephone. As the woman charged with reaching out to the Irish-American community for Senator Obama, Wheeler was juggling ten different tasks a day – no, make that twenty. She would need a phone bank to make calls into crucial battleground states, more people out canvassing in Virginia, plus extra boots on the ground in Ohio where "huge numbers of persuadable voters" had been identified. In Colorado, Wheeler had commandeered "another Irishman" – Denver's city auditor – to help Obama there, and whenever freed from scrounging for favours, she would spend evenings outlining Obama's Irish credentials to groups like the Ancient Order of Hibernians.

Carol Wheeler, a petite blonde with a bright smile, was one of the first high profile Washingtonians with Irish connections to support Barack Obama. In early 2007, Carol, a native Iowan, and her husband Tom invited the young senator to their home for a fundraising dinner. What drew them initially to Obama was his memoir *Dreams from My Father*. "Arguably that book had more of an impact on politics in this country than any other book you can name in recent memory," Wheeler said, referring to how readers began to comprehend the remarkable story of Barack Obama's life. Written when Obama was in his thirties, the book had by November 2008 been on the *New York Times* best seller list for two years. Reading about Obama's struggle to find his own identity and how he dealt with race, Wheeler felt Senator Obama was someone she wanted to see in the White House. "I mean, this is one smart guy," she said, recalling that the first thing she noticed about him was how intently he listened to others. "Barack Obama is usually the smartest person in the room, but he doesn't feel the need to make that clear continually," she said.

Known mainly for her work with both Protestant and Catholic children from Northern Ireland, Carol Wheeler reached out to Irish-Americans on Obama's behalf – a job the candidate himself made easier by choosing Joe Biden as a running mate. "There was just an instant comfort level on the part of the traditional Irish vote," said Wheeler, referring to Biden's ability to connect with white working-class voters in pivotal states like Virginia, Ohio and the "Keystone State" of Pennsylvania.

With Hillary Clinton now putting in long hours on the stump for Barack Obama, Clinton's former Irish supporters, including Stella O'Leary, followed suit. Niall O'Dowd's *Irish Voice* likewise endorsed the Democratic nominee. "After a brief stumble on the issue of the special envoy, Barack Obama's campaign has clearly become far more responsive to the Irish-American community," O'Dowd's paper said, adding that

Obama would send an "eloquent signal to the world that America has made a fresh start".

There were signs that the broader Catholic vote was changing too. Though Republicans had tried to pry Catholics from the Democratic fold using moral or so-called wedge issues, smaller numbers of the faithful were now willing to vote for a president on the single subject of abortion. "It's not to say that Catholics are indifferent on the issue," said *Los Angeles Times* columnist Tim Rutten. "It's just that they decline to make it the single topic on which they vote." A Georgetown University survey found that in 2008 only one in five Catholics felt morally obliged to take direction from either American bishops or even from the Pope when deciding whether to vote Democrat or Republican.

NEAR THE SMALL TOWN OF TROY in western Ohio, Roger Kearney, a descendant of Protestant Irishmen, was also counting the days to 4 November. Not only did he intend to cast a ballot for a candidate he believed would change America, seventy-two-year old Kearney planned to vote for his cousin Barack Obama. "Fourth cousin, three times removed," Kearney said, explaining that the web of presidential connections stretched all the way back to Moneygall, County Offaly and Barack Obama's Irish great-great-great-grandfather.

Roger Kearney, a retired technology director who enjoys poking around family history, read in 2007 about Barack Obama's Irish ancestry and was immediately struck by the name Fulmuth Kearney. "I thought, 'I know who that is. I've got him in my database'," said Kearney, who sent his information to the genealogist working on Barack Obama's Irish lineage and discovered that it all matched up. He and the presidential candidate shared a common ancestor, Joseph Kearney, back in County Offaly in the eighteenth century. "I was amazed," he exclaimed, stressing he had been a keen supporter of Barack Obama since hearing his address to the 2004 Democratic Convention. "I said, 'That young man is going to run for president some day, and I intend to vote for him'."

In Kearney's heavily Republican part of Ohio, the Obama family link was not universally celebrated. "Several have been amazed that I haven't tried to hide it," Kearney told me, adding that he received a few funny looks and unsavoury comments after breaking the news to friends and neighbours. In the mainly white area north of Dayton, many Ohioans, he suspected, had never spoken to an African-American. "The only black people they really know are the ones they've seen in crime stories on television," Kearney stated, adding that most folks softened as they began to learn more about Obama. "I tell them he's as Irish as I am. That gives them pause. They just think about that for a moment," Kearney said. On voting day, the blood relationship would be secondary to Roger Kearney. Politically, he felt the same way about Barack Obama, regardless of their common ancestry. "I think he is going to approach everything from a smarter perspective," Kearney went on, hoping that President Obama planned to sit down and negotiate with the Republicans in Washington as a way of easing the partisan bitterness gumming up the wheels of power. "Perhaps they can come up with some good ways of doing things."

With two weeks remaining in the longest election campaign in history, the Obama team had combined relentless preparation with a measure of "Obama Luck" to reach a position of quiet confidence. Their good fortune had been the timing of the autumn 2008 economic crisis. On 14 September, one day before the global financial earthquake hit Wall Street, Barack Obama called his staff together at their Chicago headquarters. Obama was worried that his campaign was going stale. McCain's running mate Sarah Palin was hoovering up the media coverage, and Obama's message on the economy was not getting through. The next day, however, the crumbling economy became the story, and Obama was primed to take advantage of the new opportunity.

The vigorous preparation that allowed Obama's team to glide self-assuredly to the finish line produced two results which helped seal his victory. In September, Obama's money machine collected a stunning $150 million in donations, allowing for a final advertising blitz in contested states, most of which were traditionally Red. With the exception of Pennsylvania and New Hampshire, John McCain abandoned any hope of winning Blue states from the Democrats and put his smaller financial cache to work defending states that George W. Bush had won in 2004. Republican states McCain was in danger of losing to Barack Obama included Iowa and Ohio in the heart of the country, North Carolina in the mid-Atlantic region, Florida in the south, the western states of Colorado, Nevada and New Mexico, as well as the "Old Dominion" state of Virginia which had been reliably Republican since 1968. "Obama's money advantage forced McCain to make tough choices about where to compete," said Massie Ritsch of the Center for Responsive Politics in Washington DC. "It forced him to compete in places Republicans traditionally hadn't needed to."

Obama's $700 million haul broke all records for election fundraising. While a larger number of donors gave smaller amounts, the number of Americans who contributed to the 2008 election still represented no more than about 4 per cent of the population. "Even at the three million donors his campaign

claims, Obama had just one per cent of the population contributing," Ritsch said. By election day, the CRP estimated that
$2.4 billion was spent on the presidential campaign, as well as
an additional $2.9 billion on House and Senate races. The total
of $5.3 billion, however, was still less than what Americans
spend on potato chips in a single year!

Obama's strategy of round-the-clock voter registration paid
off too. In Florida, an extra 400,000 were added to the voting
rolls, and in Virginia the number added was half a million. But
the real benefit to Obama was the huge proportion of these
new people who identified themselves as Democrats. In Pennsylvania, 430,000 new Democrats registered, many of them
young people or minorities, compared to 175,000 Republicans.
In North Carolina, 175,000 first-time Democrats signed on to
the voting rolls, outstripping first-time Republicans by three to
one. To cope with the larger number of Americans fulfilling
their civic duty in 2008, several states opened polls ahead of
time to avoid long voting lines.

Six days before the election, the Obama campaign aired a
$3 million political message that ran for thirty minutes on all
the major television networks. If voters were still sitting on
the fence, this slick Hollywood-produced promotion was designed to nudge them right off it. Focusing on the struggles of
working families, Obama promised that help was on the way.
Even if it was not, the sight of the candidate with his arms
around the shoulders of factory workers or sympathising with
small business owners was reminiscent of Bill Clinton. "People
now feel more anxious about an unregulated market, rather
than an over-weaning government," said Peter Beinart, senior
fellow with the Council on Foreign Relations, commenting on
how John McCain and "Joe the Plumber" had failed to win

over enough swing voters with warnings of impending Democratic income redistribution. "We're already undergoing income redistribution in America. It's from the middle to the top," journalist Tim Rutten added.

That was the sentiment I got while driving through the pure Red state of West Virginia – where fear of a complete economic disaster had changed some minds about traditional politics. "They were hardheads down here, but they are turning," said Al, a tough-looking old man sitting on his stoop taking in the evening sun in the town of Martinsburg. It was Saturday, and town had just held its autumn parade. But Martinsburg's Main Street had cleared, and the town was dead. The only figures on the street were the Halloween ghouls hanging from every lamppost. Shops were open, but no one was doing business. Assistants at the Deja Vu women's clothes shop looked out the window, and I did not see a single customer inside the Spring House Restaurant, where the $3 dish-of-the-day was "Chipped Beef and Gravy over Toast".

For all this, Martinsburg was not the hardest hit of the small towns you will find in West Virginia. There is a train station here, and the Internal Revenue Service has a large centre to process America's electronically filed tax returns. Other good-paying jobs like coal mining have gone, and farming in the lush fields of the Blue Ridge valley has slowed. In Martinsburg, the median income for a family is $36,000 per year, and one-fifth of the community lives below the poverty line – many of them young people who have no hope of living as well as their parents did in the 1980s.

Tiny Miracle Miller, I guessed, to be about sixteen years old, but she said she was twenty. Miracle's freckled face and long auburn hair gave her a Celtic look. She smoked a cigarette and

216

held the hand of Andrew Pennington, a boy who wore a green rocker-t and a silver earring. I almost let them pass by, but they were the only people on the sidewalk. Yes, they would definitely be voting – and for Barack Obama. Miracle and Andrew were engaged to be married, but they could only afford a gold band. There would be no diamond, at least not yet. Both had jobs, but they were not well paid. "People are talking about going back into a depression. We're really struggling with it," Miracle said, telling me that she and her fiancé rented an apartment and were stretched to pay for all the things a young couple needs. "McCain is going to tax health care, and I don't like that," Andrew said, referring to the thousands of dollars that some employers contribute tax-free toward workers' health plans. "Obama seems like he's more for the underclass than McCain," he added. Barely out of school, Miracle Miller and her future husband already saw themselves as part of America's "underclass". Unlike most of their fellow West Virginians, however, Miracle and Andrew refused to vote on traditional Red state issues like patriotism, guns and religion. None of this would put money in their pockets. The young couple would be casting their very first votes with their economic future in mind.

Dan, a middle-aged man in a lumberjack shirt who had made too many fast food runs, was not planning to vote at all – one of approximately 45 per cent of Americans who would skip the long lines on polling day and never know the difference. "I got my own business. I ain't done nothin' for six months or more," he said, adding that his job was to "haul trash". Real estate companies hired Dan to clean apartments when tenants moved out, but no one had called him in a while. These days, Dan drove around in his truck, totally dependent on a small disability payment and looking fed up.

"I'm not interested in politics this year," he sighed. "But if I was, it wouldn't be Obama." Desperate Dan walked off past the ghouls and goblins up Martinsburg's empty Main Street. It was clear he did not expect hope to come knocking anytime soon.

DESPITE EARLY INDICATIONS THAT Obama would make major gains across the electoral map, his volunteers in the Blue state of Pennsylvania were leaving nothing to chance. Located in an old red-bricked warehouse in Lancaster, Obama headquarters was a warren of activity. "Make as many calls as possible. Be accurate. Be persuasive," read the motto on the wall, where volunteers of all ages and colours tried to encourage strangers to vote for Obama. These "phone-bankers" were just the tip of the volunteer structure. Sheets of paper pasted on the warehouse walls contained the names, numbers and emails of people ready to canvass neighbourhoods or drive voters to the polls on election day. From floor to ceiling, it was volunteer wallpaper.

Just as in the primary contests eleven months earlier, Obama campaigners closed their ears to opinion polls – even those showing their own candidate with a comfortable 10 per cent lead. "We don't listen to the pollsters," said Joyce, a flaxen-haired woman who looked as if she needed a break from her desk. "I'm still too worried about the western part of the state," she added, indicating an enclave of working-class Pennsylvanians who would likely side with Sarah Palin's claim that Democrats were planning a socialist America.

As the marathon campaign came to a close, the candidates kept up a physically draining schedule – holding rallies in three separate states a day and grabbing sleep in between on campaign planes. On their final day, John McCain and Sarah Palin hit a total of eleven states between them. Barack Obama, who aides said rarely paused to eat while making his case, split seven states with Joe Biden. At a rally in Florida on election eve, Barack Obama received news that his eighty-six-year-old grandmother had lost her battle with cancer. Madelyn Dunham, who helped to raise Barack as a teenager in Hono-lulu, was just a day short of seeing her grandson make it to the White House. "She has gone home," Obama said, before con-tinuing on to the last stop of the campaign that had shaped and tested him since January 2007. Aides later remarked that the months spent sparring against Hillary Clinton had been the most intense for Obama. John McCain was the easier opponent.

"WHAT TIME IS IT?" CLARENCE SHIELDS shouted up Lexington Street on the afternoon of 4 November 2008. "Obama time!" a girl named Taz yelled back to him. Everyone passing by laughed, so Clarence and Taz shouted to one another again. The busy streets around Lexington Market belong to Baltimore's Af-rican-American community. The indoor market sells fresh fish, vegetables and inner-city cuts of meat such as oxtail, pig's trot-ters and hog jowls. The market's sushi counter accepts food stamps. By mid-afternoon, everyone I met there had already voted for Barack Obama, many having set out for the polls be-fore sunrise. "It was crowded at quarter-to-six," reported one woman, who planned to beat the morning rush but ended up standing in line with several hundred other voters. "It felt good," said Sheila Lindsey, who got her three sisters to the polls but not her mother, who, history or no history, would not budge even for Obama. "My mother is a Hare Krishna. She believes the political government is the devil's work," Lindsey said.

"Go rock the vote, y'all!" Taz gave another roar up the street. The mother of three knew all about getting people to the polls. She used to work for a voter registration company, but until today she had never voted herself. "I took my oldest child. I allowed her to press the button for Barack Obama," Taz said proudly. "It's a time in history I can share with my children." Sam Jones also pulled the lever for the first time, though he appeared to be nearly sixty years old. Sitting in a wheelchair in the doorway of a disused store, Sam looked as if he needed "Change", but he was settling for the symbolism of the day. "My ancestors came to America as slaves. Some of them died violent deaths," he said, looking at me with the saddest brown eyes that contained the pain of generations past and present. "I thank God for this day," Jones said.

"We know he can walk on water, but where are the loaves and the fishes?" Democratic strategist Donna Brazile had once said about Barack Obama. As his victory came close enough to touch, the burden of what lay ahead was already weighing not just on Obama himself, but on all who had elevated him to the status of supreme dream-keeper and "Hope" carrier-in-chief. Obama would inherit a deepening recession, two military conflicts, a decaying national infrastructure and a demoralised American middle class. The list of foreign policy conundrums alone would keep any president busy for years. There were Afghanistan, Pakistan, Iraq and Iran for starters – as well as the ascent of China. "I'm scared about the portfolio the next president will inherit," said Steven Clemons of the New America Foundation, adding that the new administration would have to quickly define America's goals. "The world doesn't know when we are going to deploy power, what our priorities are, what we are willing to gamble on, and what we care about.

You are going to have a lot more big players testing America, creating a crisis to see how we react." Though President Obama can count on less public hostility from overseas, American experts predict he will not court popularity for its own sake. "He's going to want to improve America's image with an eye to being able to get other countries to do certain things," said Peter Beinart of the Council on Foreign Relations. In Germany, Obama had already signalled to Europe that more troops would be needed in Afghanistan to bring that region under control.

Back home, the challenges will be no less daunting. Managing certain economic decline might quickly dampen the heady enthusiasm that fuelled his campaign. Even with a reassuring Democratic majority in both the House of Representatives and US Senate to aid him, President Obama will still have to find ways to tow along the wounded Republicans. "At its core, this is still a center-right country," said Greg Valliere, chief political strategist with the Stanford Group, who believed Obama's greatest asset in hard times would be his ability to speak honestly to people. "You go back to FDR, and it was just about giving people some reason for hope. That's Obama's strong suit. Maybe it's ephemeral. But I think initially, at least, he's going to make people feel better."

Linda Randle was not expecting any overnight miracles from the new man in the White House. Though she had known Barack Obama when he had first come to Chicago to work with her and others in their South Side neighbourhoods, she believed that even the best community organisers would need assistance from the communities they aspired to serve. "As African-Americans, we're going to have to step up our game too," Randle said. "He doesn't have a magic wand. He won't be able to change a lifetime of things that have gone wrong."

As the results rolled in, Obama staffer Jacob Klein was watching tallies on a television at the field office in Coral Gables, Florida where he had spent many late nights. Virginia was not yet showing a substantial lead for Obama. Klein was getting fidgety, so he walked out to move his car. A twenty-nine-year-old video editor originally from California, Jacob Klein had made the transition in March 2008 from a volunteer to a full-time campaign employee charged with getting out the vote. "At the car, I got a text message. Fox News had called Ohio for Obama. At that moment, I knew there was no chance John McCain would be elected," recalled Klein afterwards. "It was the greatest night of my life – the relief that we had taken back our country."

To Jacob Klein, working with the Obama campaign had felt like being "part of an insurgency", particularly during the primaries. On his first weekend volunteering, Klein arrived about midnight at a New Hampshire farmhouse to find the door open and a welcome note. "There was such trust, this instant camaraderie, like we were citizens in an underground volunteer army," he said. Since then the campaign had taken Klein from Philadelphia, to West Virginia, to Georgia, and finally to the battleground state of Florida, which President George W. Bush had so controversially won in 2000 and retained in 2004. In 2008, however, Florida was one of the many states that flipped to Obama. "A big change is that a lot of young Cubans are no longer single-issue Republican voters," Klein confirmed, noting that jobs and health care became more important than anything the Castro regime was up to back in Cuba.

Though he was not assigned to the campaign's Chicago headquarters, memorable events affected Klein's day-to-day operations, not the least of which was the selection of Sarah

Palin as John McCain's running mate. The choice hit Klein as "a recklessly unqualified pick" – an example of "politics over policy". "A lot of volunteers came to us and said it was the Palin pick that made them double-down for the last two months. She definitely brought some added passion to our side," recalled Jacob Klein. McCain's tactic of suspending his campaign in late September was an event Obama's team did not quite understand. "He didn't suspend his campaign. All his field offices were open. He was still running ads." Both the Obama and McCain camps agreed that McCain's wobbling had shifted the momentum to Barack Obama. As the candidates' contrasting leadership styles became apparent, staff back at Obama headquarters combed the dictionary looking for a phrase to describe John McCain. They came up with "erratic". It stuck.

Just like so many Americans moved to act in 2008, Jacob Klein spent a full year working sixteen hours a day for a man he had shaken hands with only once in a crowd. "I feel like I know him," Klein said of Obama. "He has changed my life." In a subsequent conference call with staff, Vice-President-elect Joe Biden congratulated everyone for running the most organised presidential election campaign he had witnessed in all his thirty-five years in politics. "In some ways it was total chaos," admitted Klein, who ran a busy Miami office marshalling volunteers, registering new voters and getting people to the polls. Printers broke down, spreadsheets got lost, but as Jacob Klein saw it, the long campaign was evidence for Obama's argument that politics is about more than policy papers and positions. Obama proved it is also about the "animating spirit of hope and optimism" and "Yes we can". "It produced real results in the real world. That's the force that kept us moving forward," Klein concluded.

Michelle Cooper was speechless by the time Barack Obama crossed the 270 Electoral College vote threshold the candidate required to officially become the forty-fourth president of the United States. At an election night event in downtown Baltimore, everyone around her was going crazy, and I thought I might have to hold upright the pretty black woman in the red dress, in case she fainted. "Oh my God!" she cried. "Can you believe it?" Big tears flowed freely down Cooper's face, and in a way I felt like I had intruded on her moment of history. "Oh my God! Oh my God!" she sobbed.

"USA! USA! USA!" chanted the mixed crowd of about a thousand Baltimore revellers. "Yes he did! Yes we did!" they shouted above the Stevie Wonder song "Signed, Sealed, Delivered, I'm Yours" that was ringing out all around us.

Beside Michelle, Christine Williams was crying too. "I didn't think it was possible in my lifetime, even though I'm only thirty-eight," she said. Christine felt satisfied that her children and grandchildren would not have to grow up thinking there were limits to what they could achieve. That day was gone. "I would have voted for Barack if he was white and John McCain was black," said an African-American girl called Keneisha, stressing that race had not been the issue for her in this election. Obama was simply the better candidate. After all the soul-searching about whether or not America would elect a black president, the returns showed that fears about racial prejudice at the ballot box had not materialised. Those bothered by skin colour had either voted for the other candidate or stayed at home. People claimed to have been more concerned by John McCain's age than by Barack Obama's skin colour, a signal that America had taken a critical leap towards accepting diversity at the top.

"The things I can do are endless!" exclaimed Darryl Greene, a burly man who edged his way through the crowd with his young daughter. "Bobby Kennedy said four decades ago that in forty years we would have an African-American as president. We are standing on so many folks' shoulders to be able to get to this space right here," Greene said. A team of stern-looking bodyguards cleared a path for Baltimore's mayor, who had broken some barriers of her own. Sheila Dixon is a petite black woman who, in an often dangerous city, is as much crime-fighter as politician. "Barack Obama started as a community organiser in an urban city, so he understands what urban communities need," Dixon commented, before being guided backstage by her posse.

For my husband and me, the walk back to our hotel that mild November night was filled with hoots, hollers and high-fives from strangers. It was one of those evenings when the walls that separated people came down, and we all mingled like we were the best of friends. If this was change, it felt good. Maybe this time, we can build on it before barriers creep up again. Back at our hotel on Pratt Street, groups gathered around televisions in the lounge were waiting to hear Barack Obama speak at Chicago's Grant Park. The picture cut to celebratory scenes from Times Square as well as to Kenya, where Africans in Obama's ancestral homeland were dancing and singing their hearts out for the man they claim as theirs too. In Moneygall, I dare say, the locals were smiling broadly.

As President-elect Barack Obama walked forward on the Chicago stage with his wife Michelle and daughters Malia and Sasha, a tall African-American man leaned back against the wall near me and let out a long happy sigh. "Unreal," I heard him say. "This is just unreal."

Index